DANGER!

Three Jewish Peoples

DANGER!

Three Jewish Peoples

by
Avraham Avi-hai

SHENGOLD PUBLISHERS, INC.
New York

ISBN 0-88400-164-4
Copyright © 1993 by Avraham Avi-hai; Henrietta Wagner Avi-hai
Library of Congress Catalog Number: 93-085300

Published by Shengold Publishers, Inc.
18 West 45th Street
New York, NY 10036

Printed in the United States of America

Dedication

For my daughters who have been my teachers:
Shoshana Levinson,
Tova Avihai-Kremer
Drorlee Reiner.

Acknowledgments

The author wishes to thank the following friends who encouraged him in many ways to persevere:

Laris and Leon Cohen, Jerusalem;

Louise and Murray Cornblum, Toronto;

and the Hollander Foundation

as proposed by Camilla and Fritz Hollander, Stockholm.

Henrietta Avi-hai provided constant encouragement and insight. Amnon Hadari and Jonathan Shiff assisted in research and editorial efforts. Moshe Sheinbaum understood the need for this book. Kalman Sultanik, as usual, displayed constant friendship.

These and other friends and colleagues who urged that the book appear, merit gratitude, especially one who followed this work almost from its inception, and rekindled enthusiasm. The writer alone bears responsibility for its content.

CHAPTER ONE

THE VIEW FROM JERUSALEM

There is a new Jewish people being born in Israel. Israeli Jews are different from Jews elsewhere. They are not only different from the Jews of the modern Diaspora—wherever they may live outside of Israel—they are also different from the ultra-orthodox in Israel and abroad.

The founders of Israel naturally used the national definition of their Jewishness. The founding Zionists, mainly from the former Czarist empire and its immediate neighbors, were to be bolstered by immigrants from the Middle East. To a great extent Jews in the Arab and Muslim lands as well saw themselves as a separate people, and though different from their Ashkenazi brothers in many ways, both groups were "natural" *national* Jews.

Both shared a common culture and calendar, common languages, a common history, and a sense of unity of destiny and fate. They lacked only one characteristic of other nationalities. They lacked a land, a territorial base. In this sense, the Israeli people is a continuation of a major stem of Jewish history: pre-Holocaust Eastern European Jewry.

These Jews in the stretches of Eastern Europe and of the Middle East knew automatically that they could never be Russians or Poles or Romanians or Iraqis or Egyptians. The majority of them did not even wish to be Russians or Poles or Iraqis or Egyptians. A Jewish state was a natural extension of their perceptions.

For Jews who emigrated to the West, the story is altogether different. To achieve equality, they embraced another culture, calendar, internal clock, civil religion. They defined themselves as Americans of the Jewish faith, or as just American Jews, or as British Jews, French Jews.

Except for tiny enclaves which huddle together and breast the stream of the assimilating powerful current of day-to-day life, they have lost their languages and their rhythm of life. Furthermore, their lives are not at stake as Jews. Every Israeli's life is. Good or bad, this reality, and the others—those of language, culture, calendar, civil religion, politics—create a distinct person, a distinctive people.

The creation of this people marks a watershed. The Diaspora and especially American Jewish communities are based on other premises, live a vastly different life, march to another drum.

And, everywhere in the world, in Israel, the Americas and Europe, in Australia and even the Far East, world-wide ultra-orthodox Jews march to their own beat, live in their own cocoon.

The Jewish people we have been for so long is becoming three Jewish peoples. This book comes to say how and why. It also warns against a schism which may be irreparable.

This lesson was taught to me originally by my own family. Because I came to Israel from Canada, I can never be a *sabra*, a native-born Israeli. My three daughters were born in Israel: they are *sabras*. Now grown women, each fills multiple roles as wife, mother and career woman. All three have been my teachers. As they were growing up, I tried to understand their life realities. Not only what distinguished each from her siblings, made each one unique, but also what distinguished them from me, a Canadian-born son of Jewish immigrants from Poland.

My move to Israel, I felt, deprived my daughters of only one thing—the presence of grandparents and the extended family. So, effort and expense notwithstanding, their mother and I took them as often as possible for family visits to Canada. The trips were not infrequent, the reunions warm and satisfying. I came to realize however that my children and my sisters' children, separated for only a few years at a time, had less and less in common. Once the family bonds were reviewed and reknotted, I could see that what my children had experienced in their lives was not understood by their first cousins. What my nephews and nieces experienced was not relevant to my children. Immense currents of Jewish history had washed over Canadian Jews without deeply affecting their lives, whereas my daughters were living within the heart of Jewish history, at the pulsebeat of Jewish life.

Mass culture and instantaneous communications change people rapidly. Change itself has changed: it has accelerated. The thought patterns of my grandparents in Poland, their values and life realities were essentially similar to those of Jews who lived hundreds or even thousands of miles away, and hundreds of years earlier. Yet my children, and my nephews and nieces—in the span of merely one generation—were on the road to becoming members of two separate Jewish peoples.

My path in Israel led me to government and public service. As a result, I visited every major Jewish community, and many smaller ones in the Western world: Helsinki and Johannesburg, Melbourne and Madrid, Buenos Aires and Berlin. My studies and travels in the United States took me from Mobile, Alabama to Syracuse, New York, from Boston, New York and Miami to Los Angeles, San Francisco and San Diego.

What I saw reinforced what I had learned from my daughters. This was doubly reinforced when I taught overseas students at Israeli universities, North American students in the U.S. and Canada, and then Israeli students in Israel. I discovered again and again that although my daughters speak English perfectly, yet, as Israelis, we do not speak the same language as Diaspora Jews.

Whether interpreting Israel to the Diaspora or explaining the Diaspora to Israel, I found I was dealing with what was becoming— or even more alarming, what had already become—two different peoples.

Nor was the Jewish people simply splitting into two neat halves. As the "old" schism between ultra and not-so-ultra-orthodox Jews deepened, this cleavage became more marked, sharper. It became clear that there was yet a third group, apart and isolated from the others. These are the ultra-orthodox who give primacy to *Halachah*, the divinely revealed Law as transmitted through their rabbis and who do not admit any other value to exist alongside of it.*

For me, this division of the House of Israel cut particularly close to home. Once a fully observant orthodox Jew, I no longer classify myself as such, though I do practice many of Judaism's basic customs and rules. Still, I object to labels and divisiveness. When I was still an obser-

---

* Academics may be uncomfortable with the transliteration used here. I prefer a simple phonetic system which looks less strange to the eye: e.g. "halachah" instead of "halakha."

vant "orthodox" Jew, I had acted on behalf of the Prime Minister of Israel to help introduce the Conservative and Reform seminaries and their World Centers into Jerusalem. This I did as a conscious "catholic," i.e. universal, all-embracing and unlabelled Jew, who believed that Israel belongs to each of us. It was an action that was in line with our Declaration of Independence which guarantees freedom of religion.

While I was doing this, my daughters attended modern orthodox schools and youth movements. This was a conscious decision, and all the while I just as consciously tried to direct them away from an evolving narrowness and conformism which I feared would lead to chauvinism and to authoritarian political and religious practices. I saw Western culture and democratic values as a natural complement to their innate Jewishness.

Our lives were in microcosm a laboratory of the national macrocosm.

The religious issue acquired a new perspective when I remarried. My second wife is from the United States. Her adjustment to Israeli reality required her to adapt her own traditional Jewish upbringing to the secular/religious chasm in Israel which separates Jew from Jew. From her I learned what it means to be a parent of sons born in Israel, boys who may one day be called upon to risk more than my girls had to risk when they served in the Israel Defence Forces.

Thus it was from careful and empirical observation that I came to the conclusion that we may no longer be one people at all.

Why is that important? What difference should this make to others, to non-Jews and Jews alike?

The existence of the Jews affects all mankind. Beginning with the Bible, the Jews have had an overwhelming impact on Western civilization; their role within it is fundamental and crucial. The Church in all its variations cannot remain indifferent to the Jews, both because Christianity must acknowledge the source of its birth and then somehow relate to the ongoing existence of Judaism.

A. M. Cioran, who has been called the most outstanding writer in French of this generation opens an essay on the Jews with these words:

> I shall set out to describe the sufferings of a people, [to write]
> of its experiences which challenge history, of its destiny which

4

stems, so it would seem, from a supernatural logic in which the unbelievable is interspersed with the certain, miracle with necessity.*

But even for those who are indifferent to the Bible and its role in world civilization, and to the "supernatural logic" of the Jewish experience until 1939, the Holocaust served to make the Jewish people a central issue in the history and conscience of mankind.

Media attention focuses on Israel to a degree that is totally disproportionate to its size. There is an almost perverse preoccupation with Jews. The mystery of the Jews and their continued existence, their eminence in the arts and sciences, their innovations in wide areas of modern life capture the imagination—and all too often, the fear, jealousy or hatred of mankind. Therefore, simply put, the human race would be less human without the Jews. Any major change in the Jewish people as it has been known through the ages would be an upheaval in the ordering of the world. If this holds for the world, how much more so for Jews. No matter how sketchy their Jewish observance, their identity or allegiance, Diaspora Jews ask a series of questions about themselves, questions often asked with a sense of dread.

"Will there be a Jewish people outside of Israel a century from now—fifty years from now? What kind of people will we be? Or at the very least, will my children or grandchildren be Jewish?" This is the central Jewish concern for Jews who care about being Jews, and who live outside Israel. These are the questions which causes sleepless nights. In the background is the sense of loss, of change. In the past half-century the Jewish people have undergone changes which beggar any adjective. These developments make the Jewish people as it once was almost unrecognizable. If present trends continue—and that is a very

---

* This quotation is taken from "A People of Individuals," by A.M. Cioran, as translated by Yehoshua Kenaz into Hebrew, *HaAretz*, Tel Aviv, September 19, 1990, p. B4 ff. The reference to Cioran's role in French literature is from "An Honorary Jew," by Yoram Bronowski on the same page. My translation suffers from being filtered first into Hebrew, since the original was not at hand as I wrote.

large "if"—we seem to be witnessing the end of the one Jewish people, and the birth of three Jewish peoples.

THE THREE

The largest "people" by far is composed of those non-orthodox North American Jews who live a lifestyle unlike any known in the past.[1] Their world, their day-to-day reality, their dreams and hopes, their symbols and role models are unique: so unique that they are becoming a new and different people. They are different from their grandparents who came to North America, different as well from their cousins in Israel, but also clearly different from the ultra-orthodox in the United States and elsewhere.

A second Jewish people is evolving in Israel. They are a people who do not believe that Jewish religious law is binding, or that orthodox rabbis have a monopoly on its application. It is a people whose lifestyle is therefore secular; they range from anti-orthodox, atheist or agnostic to the traditionalists who preserve some forms of religious observance but do not live by the total rhythm set by rabbinic authority. The lifestyle, language, and day-to-day reality of this evolving secular people is as far removed from their non-observant American cousins as it is distant from those of their grandparents or even the secular founding fathers of Israel.

The third evolving Jewish people is the ultra-orthodox. Strictly observant Jews share a common universe of discourse, common realities and problems, and a common world view. In spite of the many rifts within this body, they call themselves the *Torah Camp*: they believe in the binding nature of a Divinely revealed Torah. This belief expresses itself in rabbinically authorized observance which embraces the totality of their existence and determines the rhythm of their lives. In many cases, it also places limits on the scope of their intellectual pursuits. Ideologically they are basically anti-Zionist and range from active opposition to Zionism and Israel to passive acceptance.

This three-way division does not include in any detail Jews living in Western countries outside North America. The omission is deliberate. Important as they are, and regardless of the size of their communities, at this stage of history they do not seem to be a determinant in the Jewish future.

Nor have I included the former Soviet Union or the rest of Eastern bloc Jewry. In the uncharted years ahead, it is unlikely that these communities will flourish within the former Soviet empire. Today, it seems likely that a major proportion of Soviet Jewry will eventually become Israeli and some, if they can, American. The burgeoning virulent anti-Semitism in the so-called "democratizing" republics does not augur well, and as I write these lines, the flight—sometimes an exodus or even a rout—goes on. If any remain in their host countries, their fate will be a by-product of future liberalization or its reversal.

This book then is about the evolution of the Jewish people into three evolving peoples: American or Diaspora secular, Israeli secular, and world-wide ultra-orthodox. We shall look at these three in turn and try to understand what makes them different: the way they live and experience life, the national backgrounds which formed them, the way they perceive unfolding history, and how they want to see the future.

The future is not immutable, neither prescribed nor fixed in concrete. If it does not change its course as it unfolds, perhaps we may still be able to change its direction. We are becoming three Jewish peoples. The process is not yet final.

• • •

WAS THERE EVER ONE JEWISH PEOPLE?

The history of the Jewish people shows rifts and splits, assimilation and disappearance. Two kingdoms: Judea and Israel. Babylon and Jerusalem. Sepharadim and Ashkenazim. These distinctions and divisions were all branches from one root, watered by some knowledge and much practice. Until the Emancipation, one was a Jew either because he wanted to be or because he had no other choice, or one ceased to be a Jew by defection, by an act of secession: conversion. The Torah, the dream of the Restoration to Zion, the hope of Messianic times, the Holy Tongue, recalled past and dreamed future, belief in the God of Abraham, Isaac and Jacob—some or all of these gave disparate groups in our people a basic sense of unity. With all the rifts and arguments and contention, the Jews shared a sufficiently common lifestyle and faith and language to be seen by themselves and others as one people.

Since the Emancipation, Jews have been poised between assimilation and physical extinction, on the one hand, and attempts at redefinition: "religious" in the West, "national" in the East and in Israel, on the other.

The creation of Israel is a continuation of the past and also a break with the past, a Promethean, almost heretical wresting of the future from the past. It creates a rift in the present. The Nation Israel is such a strong variant within the People Israel as to endanger communication and understanding with those who choose only the "religious" definition, and shun the State. It quietly but steadily creates barriers to understanding and belonging for those in the West who adopt the "religious" definition out of conviction or convenience.

And so, as Jews disappear into their milieu, communication breaks down, interest lags, the sense of unity of destiny dissipates. History in all its future ugliness might restore Jews to Israel the nation, as happened in pre-1939 Europe and in the Soviet Union. And who wants that?

For Jews to maintain their unity, a network of filigree chains and silken cords must bind them. If that unity exists, we have a people to belong to, which will carry forward and change and evolve our Jewishness into the future, down the generations.

If the Jewish people ceases to exist as One People, as *Knesset Yisrael*—the mystic community of Israel and its expression in peoplehood—the danger of its Diaspora branches remaining alive and vibrant is overwhelming. We are not great in numbers. Our "effectives," the responsible and belonging Jews are fewer than statistics tell. The Diaspora dwindles.

Israel will continue on its path of separate nationhood. As long as Jews remain in the Diaspora, they must not—for their own sakes—lose their Jewish roots, identity and ways. For Israel's sake, and the sake of Jewish continuity, Israel needs its "hinter-people," as Chaim Weizmann called the Jews of the Diaspora. As long the Diaspora possesses cultural openness, advanced technology and democratic pluralism, it can help sway Israel in desirable directions. And the Diaspora needs Israel.

At this point, to be absolutely truthful, my Zionist faith comes into conflict with my sense of reality.

Classical Zionism held that there could be no long-term Jewish existence outside of the Land of Israel. Anti-Semitism would force the Jews to choose between emigration to Israel or remaining in Exile where hatred and assimilation would decimate them. *Galut* (Exile) and *Geulah*

(Redemption—living as free Jews in a Jewish State) are mutually in-compatible.

My heart goes with Zionism: that Galut and Geulah are incom-patible. My head, strangely, says that the Zionist analysis was particular to its time and place: Europe a century ago. Most Jews will remain wherever they are, unless they are forced to move by a turn of history which cannot be resisted. As in Newton's Third Law, they will continue in their state of rest or inertia unless made to move by an external force. A tiny minority will in the visible future choose to live in Israel. Most will not. They can therefore survive as Jews only through an act of will, that is *if they so choose and so wish.*

If they so wish, choose and act! But the battle to remain Jewish is hard in a world washed over by the mass culture which homogenizes, degrades the unique, and destroys precious divisions of culture. These divisions are not, as the 19th century liberals would have it, walls to our common humanity. They provide the separateness and uniqueness which make it possible for a people to be a people, for a person to have his individual and group identity, those values which make us more, not less human.

On a more theoretical level, there are three paradigms in play. The national existence paradigm is the Zionist paradigm: Israel is the Land of all Jews, and it will guarantee their cultural survival, growth and development. The language, the culture, the very battle over the religious or secular nature of life in the nation, the need to define the terms of co-existence in a state setting guarantee Jewish continuity and renewal.

The clash within Israel is between that national paradigm and the ultra-orthodox paradigm, that of the Jews as-a-religious-holy-people. That paradigm does not need a state, only a community at best, a ghetto at worst.

Nonetheless Jews have always chosen Galut along with Geulah. The American paradigm today is a new phenomenon: ethnic, religious and cultural distinctiveness in a free non-Jewish society. It seems possible, though difficult: Jewishness is attenuated; Jewish knowledge limited to shining small islands; Jewish numbers shrinking.

The question is whether in the American paradigm, that of common citizenship and equality before the law, there is sufficient strength for its

Jews to flourish and remain part of the Jewish people without the safeguards of strong religious observance. And then the question remains: given that some Jews will remain Jews, will they build bridges sufficiently strong to keep the sense of Oneness with the Israeli Jew? Or are the drift and breach inevitable?

• • •

If many or most Diaspora Jews elect to remain in their lands of birth, what role can Israel play for them? As American and other Diaspora Jews search for ways of asserting their identity, Israel with all its blemishes and with all its beauty, is often seen as "the answer" for their redefining and renewing their own Jewishness: a model or prototype of "total Jewish living."

WHAT AMERICAN JEWS SEEK IN ISRAEL

> "Who is a Jew? He who has a Jewish grandchild."
> (Anonymous Jewish black humor)

"Will my children and grandchildren be Jewish?" For Jews who wish to answer that question "Yes," Israel is seen as a paradigm of "Jewishness." No matter what the ambivalence towards Israel, some Diaspora Jews look to Israel to breathe life into their own Jewish identity or that of their children and grandchildren.

These come to Israel to seek their roots.

Some look for God, for a voice from the *Kotel*, the Western Wall of the Temple, the last relic of the crumbled Commonwealth of two thousand years ago.

Some look for unfettered ethnic pride: "We've been despised and killed long enough. Now we'll show *them.*"

Others search for the Jewish ethos: social justice, a new society, a great *kibbutz* of overwhelming identity and idealism.

Still others are in quest of Israel as the shining exemplar of "the Jewish brain, Jewish genius:" the cure for cancer, another Einstein, a new Isaac Stern, a reborn Leonard Bernstein, a Tel Avivian Kafka or a sabra Agnon.

Can Israel supply the answers to these needs? Certainly Israel has proven it can, somewhat, in most cases. But even in these cases, the "Israel experience" is a one-off occurrence. On returning to the reality of life in the Diaspora, the Jewish commitment gained in Israel often fades.

Yet, there is more understanding, deeper hope of communication. Helpful to thousands who do come to Israel, what does Israel have in common with the millions who never touch its soil?

On the communal level, the Israeli reality is far removed from American Jewish, British Jewish, Argentinean Jewish identity. These Jews come from pluralistic societies, or national societies of which they strive to become an integral, non-foreign part. They often see themselves, or are seen as members of a religious group, whether they practice or not, whether they observe all, some or none of the commandments.

Do they really understand the Israeli identity?

American Jews, like Diaspora Jews on the whole, see integration as an aim. Israel's very existence is a statement that integration is impossible without losing Jewish lives or the Jewish way of life. Israel is a national state of Jews, based essentially on secular nationalism, even though rooted in Jewish historic and religious values and practices, Jewish culture, Hebrew language and calendar. Israel *may* provide the seeking Jew with an intensity of Jewishness, but its form and content is not parallel to those of Jewish communities abroad.

Most Diaspora Jews see Israel through a veil of myths and slogans. These may help one's grandchild be Jewish, or "more" Jewish. It may help the community rally. But its reality is rich, convoluted, and diverse. It is less than the slogans and more than the myth. Israel is creating a Jewish people different in essence and content from anything Jews have known for two thousand years.

The growing breach between Diaspora Jews and Israel cannot be healed if one does not see this difference and understand it.

---

1. Of course, I am well aware of basic differences between the United States and Canada. The basic cultural, political and historical divergences between the two, as well as the current Canadian ideology of multi-culturalism and multi-ethnicism work well to give Jewish separateness a friendlier environment than in the US. There too, to be fair, there are important

changes under the pressure of Hispanic immigration and rising black consciousness.

Canadian Jewry, in addition, is much closer to its Eastern European and more recent Mediterranean roots. The great immigration came after World War One, in the 1920s especially, as the US clamped down on immigration, and then after World War Two. The 1950s and 1960s brought the so-called Sephardi immigration, actually mainly from North Africa and other countries, including Iran and Iraq.

Nonetheless, the face of Canadian Jews is turned southward; often their business interests and their vacation homes are in the United States. The invasion of Canadian airways by the US television stations along Canada's heavily-populated southern strip along the US border speeds Americanization of the culture. And Canadian Jewry is part and parcel of much of US Jewry's organizational life. In spite of the real differences, nonetheless, Canadian Jewry, from the point of view of this book, which is looking for broad archetypes or theoretical constructs and paradigms, is closer to the US pattern. We therefore use the term "American" as shorthand for North American.

Bernard Reisman is of this opinion as well. In "The Future of the American Jewish Community" he wrote:

This article refers to a single North American Jewish community, comprising the Jewish communities of the United States and Canada. The blending together of the Jewish communities of these two countries has been occurring over the past generation, reflecting the close relations and congruence of background and values between Canada and the United States. Also, the movement to a unitary community has been fostered by initiatives of the major coordinating bodies in American Jewish life: the Council of Jewish Federations, the Jewish Welfare Board, the United Jewish Appeal, and the organizations and seminaries of the Jewish religious denominations.*

---

* *Towards The Twenty-First Century: Judaism and the Jewish People In Israel and America. Essays in Honor of Rabbi Leon Kronish on the Occasion of his Seventieth Birthday*, Ronald Kronish, ed., Hoboken, Ktav, 1988; p. 238, footnote.

CHAPTER TWO

"SECULAR" ISRAEL

WHAT IS A "SECULAR" JEWISH PEOPLE? Can Jews exist at all in a secular mode, or is this a contradiction in terms? In Israel "secular" is an even more confusing concept. Daily life appears to have a Jewish religious coloration, far beyond the official role of (orthodox) religion in the State. Jewishness pervades the calendar: Shabbat and all the religious festivals are official holidays, so that at first sight, Israel appears to be a religious community. Indeed can one at all remove the dimension of religion from being Jewish?

To understand this Israel we must see how the majority of its Jews view themselves and express their Jewishness. Through their national days of rejoicing and mourning we see an evolving "civil religion" and national consciousness. The national "days" of a people establish national identity; they distinguish Israeli Jews from all others. Israel's national myths separate Israeli Jews from those in the Diaspora. They also mark the divide between secular Israelis and Israel's ultra-orthodox Jews.

Israel's national days—days of celebration and of mourning—mark those events which Jewish statehood has written into the calendar of the Israeli Jewish people. They penetrate home and street, school curriculum, popular culture and the media. The new State created three major new days in its national calendar, pegs on which to hang the new nation's civil religion. Only one is joyous: Independence Day. The two others, Memorial Day and Holocaust Day, are implacably sad.

INDEPENDENCE DAY: Yom Ha-Atzma'ut

Reserve duty. The soldiers in the unit are "old men," over-age for regular duties or active units. They are lying on double-decker bunks, resting. Tonight they will go out on patrol along the Lebanese border. The kibbutznik responsible for liaison with the army walks in. "I need a volunteer." For Independence Day, tomorrow, eleven o'clock, behind the kibbutz dining hall.

That evening sirens sound. The mourning of Memorial Day comes to an end. The rejoicing begins. White tablecloths in the dining hall. Special foods. Bottles of wine on every table. Folk dancing. The next day, Independence Day.

Eleven o'clock. The children file onto the lawn behind the kibbutz dining hall. Beautiful children. Large trusting eyes, sea-green or sky-blue; burning brown Holocaust eyes and black North African mellah eyes. Shabbat clothes, their best. Excited, so excited. One of the mothers whispers to the volunteer. "They can do 'attention' and 'at ease' but they can't manage the anthem. Just 'The Whole Land is Decked with Flags'. . . ."

The volunteer has shaved carefully, his uniform is pressed for the first time. His hat is on his head at regulation tilt, an Uzi hangs over his left shoulder. The children gawk and whisper and nudge one another. Overhead comes a diamond-shaped formation of four Phantom jets, screeching down the length of the border. The children lean back and gaze at the planes as they speed south, tracing Israel's borders in the sky.

The volunteer comes to the center of the square, the children form a "U" around him. Gently he says, "Parade will come to Attention. Parade. Ten-SHUN! Parade will stand at ease. Parade. Stand-AT-Ease!" Then the speech: "My name is Avraham. I am one of the soldiers who came here to help guard you." The wind sweeps across the mountaintop, distorting his voice. The sky is blue, it is a beautiful day in May, peaceful.

"Across the border," (which, he tells himself, is three hundred yards away) "there are some bad people who want to harm us." (He will not use names, inculcate hatred.) A tiny boy pipes up: "Araveem!" Arabs. Nothing secret here. Facts. "So why are we celebrating? Why have I come to be with you at this parade?" A chorus replies: "It's the birthday of the State." Prompted by their parents they begin to sing the three-word song they can manage, *Kol ha-Aretz Degalim*, "The Whole Land is Decked with Flags." Pin on the badges. Give out the candy. Beautiful children. Too young to sing the anthem, ". . . . To be a free people in our Land, the Land of Zion and Jerusalem." Not too young to know there is an enemy and soldiers and airplanes, and war.

In the cities, stages have been erected at central locations: squares, parks. Orchestras, bands, entertainers. Children stay up all night. Walk freely. Sing and dance in the street. Poke fun at their elders. Aim squeaky plastic hammers at the heads of passersby. Public figures are prime targets.

In the houses, balding men with bulging waistlines and aging women sit on chairs or spill onto the floor of crowded parlors. They retell the stories of their childhood and their youth, their wars and escapades and practical jokes. They relive the good years when we "all believed and loved and fought." Once in a while, they mention a name, and look away, not meeting each other's eye. But mostly on this night they sing the songs of their past. Sentimental songs, patriotic songs, meaningful songs. "Have faith, the day will come. . . ." Or, "next year we'll just sit out on our porch. . . ." The songs of the landmark years, vintage '48, '56, '67, '73, '82.

In orthodox Zionist homes, in orthodox kibbutzim and Zionist yeshivot, special services initiate the eve of Independence Day, including prayers composed by the Chief Rabbinate in which the the State is called "The beginning of the blossoming of our Redemption." Family meals, with Independence Day songs, and new prayers and blessings. The next morning, there are special Torah readings and the Hallel prayer of Thanksgiving: "When Israel went forth from Egypt. . . ."

Yom Ha-Atzma'ut afternoon. Houses are festooned with flags. Everywhere, people greet each other with "Happy holiday." Parks and camping sites are packed. Smoke from innumerable barbecues of spicy ethnic dishes flavor the air. Beer and wine. Families sing or listen to radios and tapes. For days before, the children have studied the 1948 War of Liberation and learned its songs.

In Jerusalem, the World Bible Quiz. Earnest Swedes and Bible-belt Americans compete with Jews from all over the world. Thousands are in the auditorium to watch. Tens of thousands tune in at home on radio or TV. All week long the media have poured out interviews, reminiscences, memories. Yom Ha-Atzma'ut. Independence Day. One day which lasts a week.

But the day before, Memorial Day, tells the other side of the story.

MEMORIAL DAY: *Yom HaZikaron*

Nothing binds a people together more powerfully than blood spilt on its behalf. What nation has not cemented its sense of purpose and unity with the precious memories of young and old who fall in battle? Each newly independent nation enshrines the powerful memory of the fallen as a rallying cry, sometimes even manufacturing folk heroes to create a Unifying Myth.

Israel's national myth is powerful. The State was born against a backdrop of bleak tragedy, the devastation of European Jewry. Lamentation for the precious kin who were wiped off the face of the earth. In Palestine, 150,000 Jewish families were locked in a battle which experts predicted they could not win. And once lost, what would remain of the saving remnant? Grief-stricken and abandoned, the Yishuv—and especially its young who were nurtured on the redeeming vision of the New Jew who is strong and free, farmer and fighter—faced the War of Liberation. This is how Israelis read their history.

The War came, the war which experts like the U.S. Secretary of State, General George Marshall, saw as impending doom for the Jews. The heads of the army-in-formation, *Haganah,* warned the pre-State proto-Cabinet that the chances were only fifty-fifty. When the fighting ended, six thousand Israelis—soldiers and civilians, men, women and children—lay dead. In the military cemeteries, teenage runners lie next to the "old" ones in their 20s and 30s, and those still older, the middle-aged who fought or were caught in the cross-fire. Male and female as God created them.

A war crowned by victory and ended by armistice agreements which were—so it seemed—a step towards peace. Jubilation and rejoicing and counting the dead. Six million a few years earlier, and now more. "In thy blood, live; in thy blood, live."*

Five armies were beaten back. "The few against the many." The Jews of Palestine: their hands tied by an arms embargo imposed by the same states which had silently let the six million go up in smoke. The

---

* This is the welcome which greets every Jewish male as he enters the Covenant of Abraham, his *brit milah* circumcision ceremony. The words first appear in Ezekiel 16:6 and are used in the Passover Hagadah family service.

Jews of Palestine: without allies, except for the young survivors pouring out of the Displaced Persons' Camps of Europe, eagerly coming "home" ready to join the fight, and a handful of Jewish and Gentile volunteers. They had small arms, tired old artillery, even some ships and planes purchased clandestinely. They had the support of their fellow Jews, important morally no less than financially.

But because they were the few and the weak, when tens of millions of Arabs—armed and advised by the West—sued for armistice, a refurbished David myth was born. This is the stuff that legends are made of. It is the echo of biblical verses such as "And one man will pursue a hundred, and two—ten thousand" [Deuteronomy 32:30]. Every child in an Israeli school, Zionist-orthodox or secular, grows up on these stories, recognizes the textures and beat of the verses even when the exact words are not remembered. Many are in scout troops and youth movements where the stories are reenacted, sometimes in dramatic nighttime games. They hike along the trails of the 1948 fighters as they explore the battlesites, committing to memory the names of campaigns and their commanders.

The media reinforces the myths. Newspaper supplements carry interviews and first-person "revelations." Television and radio do the same, sandwiching the stories between the nostalgic songs, simple, naive songs, which in the span of 40 years have become folk music.

Israel mourns. At the military cemeteries, official and private memorial services. *El Maleh Rahamim*—Lord full of mercy—sobs forth and hovers over the burial grounds like smoke rising from ancient Temple sacrifices. Parents and children, wives and lovers, friends and schoolmates visit the graves. Each mourns in his way. Some hide the glitter of unshed tears. Others weep openly, or cry out to the dead. Some keen, crouched at the graveside. Some whisper, rocking to and fro.

At eleven o'clock sirens sound across the country. Traffic ceases. The clatter of machinery is stilled. Across the country, people stand at attention. Everyone has lost someone—to war, to terrorism. In the Yom Kippur War of 1973, out of the 600,000 Jewish families in Israel, 2,400 fell. Loss of children, of siblings, of parents is an integral part of the civil religion of this newly reborn people, a nation bearing arms and facing the existential reality of life and death. There can be no Independence Day without the Day of Memory which precedes it. An Israeli day. . . .

HOLOCAUST REMEMBRANCE DAY: *Yom HaShoah**

Holocaust Day falls close to the end of Passover, when the Nazis destroyed the Warsaw Ghetto and crushed the last Jewish rebels. A day of remembering the dead, yet so different from Israel Memorial Day. Yom HaZikaron is—strange as it sounds—a "natural" occasion for Israelis: war is part of Israel's life, to be a soldier is a duty and a right. Each extended family has its own child to mourn, its own brother or sister who fell.

Yom HaSho-ah is different, and as years pass, it is less and less a memorial to specific individuals but rather to a people, a period, a culture, language, a disappeared world. True, hundreds of thousands of Israelis had family who perished in Europe. True, as well, that more than four hundred thousand survivors came to Israel. Yet can the sabra generation grasp the loss, the murder, the emptiness?

A Jerusalemite was asked to carry a gift from a neighbor to her friend in London. She sent a small packet, a trinket. . . and half-a-cigarette. The sender is today a grandmother. Can her children know the historic code, the meaning embedded in the memory of former camp inmates of that half-a-cigarette? The sabras as well as Israelis not of European ancestry usually have no first-hand memories of family killed in the Holocaust—in the "catastrophe" or the "destruction," which are the original meanings of *Shoah.*

Nonetheless, the Day is felt across the land. All places of entertainment are closed. The media interviews survivors and even perpetrators, asking, probing. A State ceremony is held at *Yad Va-Shem,* the Holocaust memorial in Jerusalem, today a focus of national pilgrimage. The Day is fully observed. Perhaps it is because the founding fathers of Israel came from the Holocaust lands. Almost every Jew in Palestine in the years before World War II had a blood relative in Europe—parents or siblings. Often the young immigrant

---

* Officially called *Yom HaShoah Ve-HaGevurah,* Holocaust and Heroism Day. "Heroism" is to commemorate the Jewish partisans and resistance in the camps and the rising of Warsaw and other ghettos.

was the sole member of the family to have reached Palestine.

This may explain the tenacity bordering on fanaticism of Israel's early fighters. They fought for family—to rescue those who could be rescued, to save those who could be saved—transcending ideology or nationalism. It was saving one's own flesh and blood.

Family has a special place in the Jewish world-view. Jews regard themselves as the descendants of Abraham, Isaac and Jacob. God Himself is referred to as the God of Abraham, Isaac and Jacob. The tightly knit family of Eastern Europe functioned as a powerful support system. The stories are legion of parents who went to the gas chambers with their children, rather than let them go alone. They are the ultimate testimony to the power of the family in the harshest of days. This is why the generation which did not know the victims mourns; why the day is so compelling for Jews who lost no blood relative in the Holocaust. Jews from Iraq or Yemen or India. The sense of Jewish familyhood makes Yom HaSho-ah everyone's family day of lamentation.

A 12-year old Jerusalem-born child. For the past year, his class has been involved in a project. Using a video camera, they have been studying the Holocaust, recording their lectures and discussions, and their visit to Yad va-Shem.

Yad va-Shem is on Mt. Herzl, once a barren hilltop. It is the highest ridge in Jerusalem and the final resting-place of Dr. Theodor Herzl, the visionary founder of the Zionist movement. In August, 1949, soon after independence, the struggling State carried out the provisions of Herzl's last will and testament and brought his bones from the "temporary" internment in Vienna to the Land—a tradition dating back to the patriarch, Jacob, and his son, Joseph, who sojourned in Egypt over three millennia ago.

In 1897, at the end of the first World Zionist Congress held in Switzerland, Herzl had written in his diary: "At Basel I founded the Jewish State. If I said this out loud today, I would be answered with universal laughter. Perhaps in five years and certainly in fifty, everyone will know it." Herzl's tomb was the first center of civil religion created by the State. In 1953, on the northwestern slope of Mt. Herzl, Israel began building the second center of civil religion, the memorial to the Holocaust, Yad va-Shem.

The youngsters saw visual displays and Nazi-filmed documentaries.

19

They saw photos of heaps of children's shoes, thriftily saved by the Aryan conquerors. They studied maps and documents. They learned that the names of the six million were being recorded there lest they remain nameless. "I will give them. . . a monument and a name [in Hebrew: Yad va-Shem]. *. . which shall not perish."* [*Isaiah* 56:5].

In the stark concrete Tent of Remembrance, the 37 children of the class held their own memorial service. They read out the names of 37 twelve-year-olds who were murdered forty-five years earlier. They wept. They filmed a record of that day, and chose for its musical accompaniment, *Lacrimosa dies illa*, This Tearful Day from Verdi's Requiem. One evening, they invited their parents to see the video. Their parents wept. Most of them, if not all, had been born after the Holocaust. Most of them—or their parents—were immigrants to Israel, from Yemen and Iraq, from Russia and North America. Wherever they come from, they see themselves as survivors.

Israel is the state of the survivors. Israel is the total state-community—and the only total community—which is heir to the thousands of destroyed Jewish communities in cities and *shtetls* of the past. It will not let them disappear from memory. Whoever takes the term "civil religion" as an *ersatz* formality, fails to plumb the depth of Israel's Jewish soul. The national days are days of passion and fervor, even when expressed in "Western" solemnity and pageantry.

Statehood made possible the creation of "official" special days to reflect new historical experience. These days are the underpinnings of Israel's civil religion. Even when endowed with a religious sense of holiness by the Zionist orthodox, the sense of God's acting through history, these "secular" days reflect Israel's experiences and concerns. They are a clustering force for Israelis on which they both form and center their national identity. As such, they are also a wall separating Israelis from other Jews.

Civil religion did not begin with statehood. Zionism had spent half-a-century prior to statehood recasting Jewish history, with the aim of forming "the New Jew"—free and independent, rooted in his own soil. The New Jew in the New Society was to celebrate the time-honored religious holidays but in line with the ideology of the movement and its reinterpretation of the past.

TRADITIONAL HOLIDAYS IN ISRAEL'S CIVIL RELIGION

The traditional religious holidays shared with overseas Jews are part of the common Jewish tradition. But since they are state holidays as well, their impact is stronger than in non-Jewish societies. Into these holidays secular Israel and its Zionist forebears and ideology have poured new meanings and fashioned distinct forms. In rejecting some of the past, its founding fathers consciously sought new content and new forms for a transformed folk religion.

But, of all the traditional holidays, there was one that no one can change, Yom Kippur. Another holiday, Pesach, has such a strong hold on the Jewish family and the folk imagination that even though specifics of its observance may change, it provides a common bond with Jews, past and present. These two, Yom Kippur and Pesach, are the most powerful occasions in the age-old Jewish calendar.

THE DAY OF ATONEMENT: *Yom Kippur*

Yom Kippur, especially the opening *Kol Nidrei* service, reduces the Jew to a child seeking his father. It binds Jews into a union with the sighs of the past and the hope of forgiveness in the future. It is a day of solemnity, of holiness and purity. It is estimated that three of every four Israelis observe the fast.* Synagogues burst with one-time-a-year worshippers, and congregations overflow into public halls which become synagogues-for-a-day. As traffic dwindles, families are able to walk to synagogue on roads that have become promenades. In Jerusalem, cars are all but nonexistent except for police and emergency vehicles.

People come in droves to the houses of prayer: less observant and non-observant, agnostics and outright atheists, there they are, especially for Kol Nidrei. Often they have embarrassed and unversed children in tow, bewildered by this annual excursion into an alien world. Twenty-four hours later, thirsty and unshaven, cheeks and eyes sunken, they return for the concluding *Ne'ilah* service to await the long blast of the *shofar* which heralds the end of the Holy Day. For many, it is also the end of holiness for the year, in the accepted religious sense (of the term).

---

* The figure predates the massive immigration from the former Soviet Union. It will be interesting to see how these immigrants adapt to Yom Kippur.

For Israelis who remember 1973, Yom Kippur stirs another set of memories. That year, the peace and stillness of Yom Kippur were shattered by wailing sirens, the herald of war, the close of an era. More than 2000 Israelis were killed and over 6,000 wounded in that war, sons and fathers, many of whom rushed out of synagogue to their units, still clad in their prayer shawls. This memory is entwined with the ancient folk memory, a day when the white robes of High Priest and ordinary petitioner alike illuminated man's purging himself of evil and turning to good. Only Yom Kippur retains its unique holiness in secular Israel.

PASSOVER: *Pesach*

Pesach, on the other hand, is a celebration. Its focus is the family and their seder meal, when the story of the Exodus, the central experience of a nation-in-birth, is retold and relived, each family according to its own traditions and melodies. Since it is centered on the family and on the national unifying myth of Exodus, on leaving the bondage of exile and entering into freedom, Pesach has an extraordinary power and a hold even on the those who are secular. Indeed, the secular sometimes conduct a rewritten seder, cast in a humanist idiom, weaving into the old texts references to the more recent past and the present.

While Passover is fully observed, the way in which it is marked varies widely. A majority seemingly abstain from bread for the entire eight-day holiday, eating the unleavened matzot in its place. But there are large numbers who unabashedly eat bread—and in a true break with tradition—do so openly at pizza counters and in restaurants. Some kibbutzim offer their members a choice of bread or matzah. Children in schools of all ideological colorations often bake matzot in outdoor improvised ovens as an act of identification with the Israelites who fled Pharaoh.

Very many Israelis refrain from any leavened product during Passover. Various ethnic groups maintain their particular traditions as to what constitutes leavening. And, oddly enough, some Jews who do not observe kashrut at all during the rest of the year, keep the Passover religious regulations in varying degrees of strictness.

Pesach strikes a special chord in Israeli Jews. So many have themselves or their parents been part of an exodus, or have witnessed Russian and Ethiopian Jews reach freedom in Israel. "The Exodus was also our experience with Germany, the modern Egypt." In Israel, liberation from bondage is part of everyday life. This "relevance" also finds its outlet in the way kibbutzim have tried to stress the biblical aspect of Pesach as the Spring Festival of rebirth on the Land.

These new forms though raise a basic problem: what is Jewishness separate from religious observance; what can be retained from the inherited tradition and what should be erased from it; what can be emphasized differently, and what can be transformed? It comes down to a question of a nationalist versus a religious interpretation of history, the role of Halachah as against the play of folk memory and ideology. Thus observance of the holidays, while bonding all Jews, has an Israel version which is a barrier separating "national" Jews (the Israeli "secular" identity) from overseas Jews (the Diaspora "religious" identity).

Israel's first Prime Minister, David Ben Gurion, was keenly aware of the two elements and their inseparable quality. "The Jewish religion is a national religion. . . . it is not easy to separate the national from the religious aspect." For him Israel's holy days had a dual meaning: "religio-cosmic" and "historic-national."

Emerging nations often develop an ideology which places new stresses on ancient history, new emphasis on reborn or recast "historical" ceremonies. In the Jewish calendar, two "minor" festivals naturally are ripe for a strongly nationalist interpretation of history: Hanukah and Purim.

THE FEAST OF LIGHTS: Hanukah

Even in the time of the Talmud, centuries after the victory of the Jews over their Syrian-Greek occupiers in 165 BCE, the Sages were leery of Hanukah. They feared that its nationalist theme might encourage rebellion against the occupiers of the day, the Romans. The Sages therefore limited and censored historical references to Hanukah in the Talmud. They stressed the religious theme of purification of the Temple from idolatry, and its rededication to the God of Israel. (The word Hanukah means rededication.) The miracle of the one lonely cruse of sacred oil which burned the entire eight days was made the focus: the military victory was barely mentioned.

The holiday is an especially popular one, and not least among non-observant or secular Jews. It is not a full school holiday, but the candle-lighting ceremonies, plays and songs in kindergartens and schools bring the holiday squarely into everyday life, and eight consecutive days of it at that. At home, there are special foods, family parties. Across the land, giant candelabra shine forth on the major buildings, while candle-lighting ceremonies are broadcast on television and radio each night and open concerts and public gatherings.

THE FESTIVAL OF LOTS: *Purim*

Purim is even more straightforward. It fits naturally into the Holocaust theme and the-whole-world-is-against-us syndrome which pervades much of Israeli life. Haman's threat of genocide is seen as a precursor to Hitler. The anti-Semitism of the story is seen as ongoing, one more justification for living in a problem-laden country. Yet Purim is a joyous time of carnival costumes and pageantry, traditionally-sanctioned hilarity, and license to drink until one cannot distinguish between a blessing and a curse. All these folk elements are embraced by various segments of the population, and the one-day holiday (stretched to two in walled cities), seems a week long.

If these holidays are so widely observed, what is the difference between the orthodox and the secular? Are not the secular simply "lapsed" orthodox? The difference is in their very essence: it is Jewish nationhood which is cast as the hero rather than Divine intervention. The secular, with a nationalist and humanist interpretation of history, have dressed these holidays in new garb. They emphasize a humanist, innovative, almost heretical observance. Celebration of God and faith are phased into the historical flow of the civil religion. Even Yom Kippur is a communion with history and a statement of Jewish "unity of destiny" rather than—or as well as—repentance and forgiveness of sins.

CIVIL RELIGION: *Archeology and Roots*

This nationalist interpretation of history leads to a search for roots in the land, a kind of deification of the past. And since Israel is a treasure trove for archaeologists, it is a way of reaching across centuries to the ancient ancestors. As one scholar said, the romantic stress on nationalism often means getting one's history wrong.

But for Israel, archeology is a surrogate religion to get one's history "right." Archeological excavations prove Israel's long tenure in the

Promised Land. The excavations are covered by the media as closely as Davis Cup or soccer finals. Thousands of Israeli and overseas volunteers have dug, dusted and labeled to uncover the direct link with Israel's ancestors. When the famous archeologist, Yigael Yadin dug the fortress at Massadah, one discovery was considered important enough to be announced by breaking into regular scheduled radio broadcasts. Hundreds of soldiers dug and used mine detectors to search out evidence of the past, or helped make camp, transport or feed the volunteers. Light military planes or helicopters flew Yadin back to Jerusalem regularly to report to the President and Prime Minister.

As part of this surrogate religion, thousands of Israeli students, soldiers and ordinary citizens hike through various parts of the country under the guidance of amateur and professional geographers and historians.

* * *

What then *is* "secular" Israel?

It is a Jewish Israel, and perhaps really should not be called secular in the narrow sense at all. "Non-orthodox" Israel, yes. A different Jewish people? It does look like it. Especially when one clearly understands the pervasive day-to-day reality of war. . . .

CHAPTER THREE

EXISTENTIAL REALITIES: WAR AND PEACE

From its birth, normalcy and peace have alternated with war and bloodshed in Israel's life. Is Israel's story that of peace punctuated by war, or of ongoing war alleviated by blessed periods of peace?

Item: From age 18, all men serve three years in the armed forces and women two years.* Until 1991 reserve duty, up to age 55, usually required a month a year. The age has since been lowered to 50. During emergencies, the reserve period lengthens.

Item: The eve of the Sabbath at main road junctions: dozens of armed soldiers—men and women—hitchhiking to their homes for Sabbath leave. In the city and town centers, armed young soldiers stroll about, chat, shop and drink coffee on their "after five" leaves.

Item: In city centers, armed soldiers and border police patrol the streets to deter terror.

Military service, an ongoing awareness of the danger of terrorist attacks, and listening to the news six or ten times a day is part of Israel's "security" syndrome. National and international events strike deeply into everyday existence. The intense reality of danger added to the collective neurosis of Jews, ("who" as Mark Twain allegedly remarked "are remarkably like everyone else, only more so") creates tremendous mood-swings.

A child born in 1967 has lived all his life in one form or another of war.

1967: Three weeks of nerve-wracking waiting from mid-May to early June. . . . Parks secretly consecrated as burial grounds for the

---

* Israeli Christian and Moslem Arabs are exempt from military service. Compulsory military service applies to Druze and Circassians; Arab Israelis may volunteer. Jewish exemptions will be discussed in the chapter on the orthodox.

45,000 possible victims should the enemy manage a first-strike bombing.

The Six-Day War: 777 Israelis killed, 2,586 wounded in battles against massive Egyptian, Syrian and Jordanian forces, bolstered by a contingent of Iraqis.

Jerusalem reunited. All of Sinai, Gaza, the West Bank and part of the Golan Heights in Israeli hands. Large numbers of reserves stay mobilized. Stunned Arab masses in the new-old "territories" and the slow beginning of terrorist acts. War of Attrition frontier incidents in the Syrian heights with casualties.

Jerusalem! The Wall, barred to Jews through most of 1900 years—or at best, limited access.

The Wall. Tens of thousands of Israelis make the pilgrimage to it. They weep and kiss its stones as did the exhausted soldiers. "We were like unto dreamers." Jerusalem. . . .

1968: A strong wave of terrorism: acts of bombing, shooting, and violence; 27 Israelis killed and 258 wounded.

1969: 25 killed and 171 wounded in terrorist acts.

1970: War of Attrition along the Suez Canal, including heavy artillery exchanges, ending with deep penetration bombing of Egypt by Israeli planes. 263 Israelis killed, 792 wounded.

A Golda Meir aphorism of times past: "We do not hate the Arabs because they wish to kill us! We hate them because our boys are forced to kill them." Under the weight of the constant struggle, even this changes.

1971: 5 killed, 45 wounded in terrorists acts.

1972: 28 killed, 112 wounded in terrorists acts.

The massacre of Israeli athletes in Munich.

1973: 1 killed and 15 wounded in acts of terror.

October: The Yom Kippur War. Any one who has not experienced the unnatural stillness of Yom Kippur in Israel, the utter tranquility in which man seems to return to an inner harmony, cannot appreciate the shock of the siren. It was not just the State of Israel that was attacked. Israelis felt their very essence was endangered, the total Jewish experience invaded.

Israel was unprepared. Grievous losses. Parents going to the front lines to search for their missing children. Parents seeking the bodies of their sons. . . .

Fathers and sons—both in uniform—meeting in the reek of cordite during battle. . . after battle. Cabinet ministers and generals whose sons fell. The desperate struggle to turn the tide: to prevent the capture of the Golan Heights which would then enable the Syrians to sweep across the plain to Haifa, to halt the massive Egyptian movement in Sinai. The counter-thrust across the Suez Canal and the encirclement of the Egyptian Third Army. News of Soviet troops on standby in Crimean airports.

Families dreading the visit, always by at least three people, "the team." At first composed of a social worker, a lawyer, and a doctor or nurse, as the number of casualties grew the composition changes: now it can include an elderly civilian, an inactive officer, a woman-soldier.

The war changed Israel's self-image and shook Israel's self-confidence. The sense of security born of belief in the infallibility of the military and the intelligence services was shaken. In the wake of the loss of innocence, an earthquake rocked Israel's political system.

Yet. . . national unity deepened. The determination of the fighters carried them to within 50 kilometers of Cairo, and thus opened the road to negotiations which would lead to the Sadat visit of 1977, to peace between Israel and Egypt.

From 1974 to June, 1982: Still more terrorist incidents, killing and wounding. Increasing attacks and *katyusha* rocketing of the northern border with Lebanon.

July 4, 1976: Entebbe. It was the high tide of anti-Israel and anti-Jewish terrorism and of hijacking, encouraged and furthered by the tacit cooperation of some European states with the terrorists. It was the low tide of Israeli morale which began when a French Airbus was hijacked to Uganda and ended with the dramatic rescue. The *selekzia* by the PLO hijackers, an echo from the past: Jews to the right, non-Jews to the left. The rescue. The mystical refrain: Six million pairs of hands carried our planes to Entebbe through the African night.

"Incidents:" a new Hebrew term, *takriot*, had to be created, almost always connoting violence and killing. Incidents mounted along Israel's northern border.

Children and parents spent night after night in below-ground shelters as shells rained across the border into villages, kibbutzim and moshavim in Galilee. In the months between July 1981 and June 1982, the PLO violated the cease-fire on 289 occasions.

1982: "Peace for Galilee."

The Lebanon War to force the PLO out of southern Lebanon "once and for all." Cabinet approval and national consensus for this limited action (originally said to be a 40 km. penetration) was amended repeatedly and stretched up to the outskirts of Beirut.

Israel became embroiled in the Byzantine twists of ethnic and religious intrigue and witnessed the killing of Lebanese by Lebanese. The tragedy of Sabra and Shatilla—hundreds of thousands demonstrating in Tel Aviv to demand that Israel pull out. For the first time in Israel's history national consensus over military action was broken. The toll for Israel was 654 killed, 4,500 wounded. The Lebanese involvement led Israelis, a people that had gone from utter and total helplessness and powerlessness to a crowning position of power and military might, to begin to appreciate the limitations of power. Soldiers returned their medals, but nonetheless grimly set about patrolling southern Lebanon, until the final pull-out in 1985, leaving a small area as an Israeli-controlled buffer zone.

From the evacuation of most of the Lebanese territory held in the war to date, terrorist incidents continued. Bombings, and attacks on civilians. From December 1987 to time of writing, Palestinian young men and women have carried out attacks on Israeli civilians. Some Arab villages and refugee camps became battle-grounds with mounting casualties as the army used force to try to maintain a semblance of order. The Intifada led to increased polarization within Israel, and a gradual hardening of the line. [The Intifada is discussed at length in Chapter 4.]

1990: The Iraqi threat.

From summer 1990 until mid-January 1991, the population waited. Would Saddam strike first? The new ABC—Atomic, Biological, Chemical: would he in premeditation or desperation use an atom bomb on Tel Aviv; would he use germ warfare; would he use gas-loaded Scuds? Psychological terror, Scud terror. Gas masks for Holocaust survivors and their children and grandchildren, gas masks and sealed rooms. Patriot missiles, Israeli self-restraint, countering all previous first strike doctrine. Jokes: A young soldier calls his Tel Aviv home from the forward positions facing the Syrians: "Hello, *Ima,* how are things at the front?" *The Israeli home front is now vulnerable.*

In the twenty-plus years since the Six Day War, children have grown up and have themselves become soldiers. To see Israel through its own eyes is to see a beleaguered state, one knowing that not only peace, but, in the final analysis, its ultimate survival—beyond diplomacy and treaties and even a total Arab-Israel settlement—depends on *its own power.*

Exegesis

Its Own Power: This means its young people are prepared to give years of their lives at a stretch, and later months of their lives for decades; to be ready to risk their lives and those of others. It means acquiring "skills" in fields not generally transferrable to civilian occupations. It means carrying out duties which can range from control of civilian demonstrations and disturbances in now overtly hostile occupied territories, to the most dangerous actions on land and sea, under the sea and in the air. To do what is necessary and "obey all legal orders." Above all, the possibility of being killed, the possibility of having to kill.

Survival: This means to continue to exist not just as a nation-state with its own distinct language and separate culture, but simply to remain alive as individuals and as a nation. It means no concentration camps, gassing or being "exterminated."

SELF-IMAGES AND UNCONSCIOUS PORTRAITS

From letters written by a 19-year-old second lieutenant to her father who was abroad, in 1974:

Dear Abba,
. . . Whenever we get home for weekend leave we go to visit Avraham's parents. Months have passed, and his body still has not been found, somewhere near the Suez Canal. The army rabbinate is searching for him. Friends from class come to see his parents any Shabbat they are in town. . . .

Dear Abba,

... Almost a year, and finally "good" news. His body has been found. Now the parents can sit *shiv'ah* and begin to return to "normalcy"....*

Dear Abba,

I dreamt about Avraham. He had his life set out for him. He wanted to be a career soldier. He knew at what age he would become company commander and battalion and brigade commander. He was going to be Chief-of-Staff by age 44.
We were at his funeral. He is the second of 17 boys who were in my high-school class. *Our class reunions now take place at the cemetery.*

A fifteen-year-old girl tells her parents: "Miri and Yaacov had a baby." The parents: "So?" "Well," comes the reply, "they named him after Yirmi!" The explanation means nothing to the parents: "So? What's so special about that?" The girl looks at her parents. Her voices changes, thickens. She fights back tears. "Miri and Yaacov and Yirmi were our counsellors in the movement. Yirmi and Yaacov were best friends. Yirmi fell in Sinai. . . . Now he has a name. . . . " Yirmi was 22 years-old when he was killed. Now again he has a name.

An American commentator, Leonard Fine wrote, "When the submarine Dakar went down some years back, with some 70 sailors drowned, an Israeli research institute learned that one of every three Israelis knew at least one of those who were lost."**

War is a pervading existential reality in Israel. It invades the psyche and soul of the very young and the not-so-young. Its effect on the horizon of life is clear. Try telling a six-year-old child not to pick up stray buttons or pencils because they may be miniature booby-traps designed for children. Try comforting a parent whose teenage daughter escaped from a bomb explosion in a bus taking her home from school—

---

* Shiv'ah (seven) is the week-long mourning which the immediate family observes from the day of burial.

**FORUM *on the Jewish People, Zionism & Israel,* WZO, Jerusalem, Winter/Spring 1989, No. 62.

with only her hearing damaged. No wonder then that a seven-year-old Israeli child crossing from France to Belgium to Holland on a car trip is amazed that there are no borders, no guards, not even immigration officials. Or is it a wonder that he asks as they drive into each country, "Are they at peace with us? Do we have relations with them? Do they have an ambassador in Israel? Do they have an army? Can we 'beat' them?"

The omnipresence of death is the other side of the coin called politics. Karl Jaspers, the late anti-Nazi German philosopher wrote: "Politics is concerned with the seriousness of power which is based on staking one's life."* Israelis recognize that living in their state means staking one's life. Underlying it is the pervasiveness of the Holocaust. And under that, the sense that "we are alone," that "the whole world is against us." This is in part the ghetto memory, fed by specific experiences and perceptions.

Ben Gurion, reviewing the War of Independence of 1947-48 said:

> Even though the two great powers in the world, America and Russia were partners in the decision [to establish Israel]. . . and even though the UN Charter. . . required its members to aid an attacked nation, not a single state lifted a finger in defense of Israel. . . .**

A perception in Israel is that no one really gives a damn whether Israel lives or dies. Ultimately Israel must fend for itself, since no one else really cares whether it lives or dies, and if Israel dies, all the Jews in Israel may die with it. And if all Israeli Jews die, the Jewish people ceases to exist.

The reader need not bother to argue the validity of the case. This is the folk wisdom of Israel, the traditional perception. Israelis can rattle off precedents beginning with Pharaoh through De Gaulle, U Thant and Kurt Waldheim. And if one counters that the U.S. is a "permanent" ally, chapter and verse will be cited for precedents about the "permanence" of

---

* *The Philosophy of Karl Jaspers*, New York, 1957, p. 59.
**Avraham Avi-hai, *Ben Gurion State-Builder*, Israel Universities Press, Jerusalem, 1974, p. 183.

such liaisons. "Being paranoid," Henry Kissinger is reputed to have said, "doesn't mean that you aren't being persecuted."

• • •

Israel's civil religion is based on an underpinning of national days and reinterpretations of traditional holidays. It embraces a search through the past for roots in the land. It internalizes the existential loneliness of the Jewish people swimming upstream, alone, often abandoned, bearing scars of holocaust and wars, terrorism and conflict.

CHAPTER FOUR

ACCEPTED IDEOLOGY: NEW REALITY

So far we have been looking at Israel's civic religion and realities of war and peace which create the prototype of the secular or non-orthodox Israel. This secularism derives from Zionist ideology. We condense a definition of Zionism into two paragraphs:

> Zionism is a political movement almost a hundred years old. Its founders realized that the progressively virulent anti-Semitism of Europe posed the threat of *physical* danger to Jewish existence while the threat of *cultural* extinction loomed, as the first flush of equality and civil rights seemed to be at hand's grasp.
>
> To preserve both the Jewish people and its culture, Zionism called for the recreation of a Jewish state in Palestine, inspired Jews to settle in Palestine and to build in every field of life and culture. The Zionist movement led the political and military struggle to achieve statehood.

With the achievement of statehood, Zionism saw its major purpose as realizing the biblical prophecy concerning the "Ingathering of the Exiles," [Jeremiah 31:8]; bringing Jews who live in the Diaspora home to the Jewish state. This is based on the belief that Jews still face spiritual extinction or physical danger.

Zionist assumptions are at the core of the school curriculum. The children are brought up with an Israel-centered world-view that underlies the teaching of all Jewish subjects. In the younger grades, children study Hebrew, Bible, and the "religious" and national holidays, together with the history and geography which relate to these subjects, from a Zionist ideological point of view. There are differences in interpretation, but these are theological.

In the State Religious ("Religious Zionist" or "National Religious") schools, Bible and religious observance are taught as the revealed word of God and as binding, authoritative Halachah. In the State ("secular") schools, they are taught as part of the "national" heritage possessed of great value and meaning, as history and folklore. Some schools, such as those in kibbutzim, or where parents wish to have an "enriched" curriculum, have special programs which emphasize labor values, or agriculture, or place a greater stress on religious topics or on national values.

Most Jewish children in Israel attend one of these school systems. (The ultra-orthodox school network is described in Section Three). Over two decades ago, Zalman Aranne, then Minister of Education, felt that the secular State school system did not teach the pupils enough about prayers, religious customs and ceremonies. A curriculum for raising "Jewish consciousness" was introduced. The purpose was not to direct children toward observing religious practices, but to prevent a break with the past, with Jewish values, and with other Jews in Israel and abroad who observed some measure of the religion.

That the secular school system needs more Jewish content is obvious to those who wish to see Jewish Israelis familiar with tradition. For example, almost every Jewish home has a *mezuzah* on its right doorpost, a third of the way from the top. In the mezuzah's container is a scribe-written parchment with a few chapters from the Torah. On the container often appears the word *Shaddai*, one of the names of God, or the first Hebrew letter of that word—SH. An Israeli-born businessman was asked to keep an appointment at a friend's home, and to save time and steps, to enter through the back door. He arrived late, and explained that he'd wandered about looking for the main entrance. When he had arrived at the back door which does not bear the family nameplate, he had not entered because "that door had the family name 'Shaddai.'"

In later grades and in secondary school, the curriculum in state schools includes world and Jewish history, along with more mathematics and science. But the ideological thrust remains the "negation of the Diaspora," a doctrine which maintains that life for Jews outside Israel leads to their being second-class citizens. "Current events," taught at all levels, reinforces this reading of history. The Jewish "lands of distress" are typified by the former Soviet Union, Ethiopia and Syria. As immigrants from these countries arrive, the object lesson for that week is obvious and trumpeted home in the media.

Its corollary truth, that in the "free countries" Jews face cultural extinction and assimilation because the Jewish component of their lives is *limited*, is also hammered home. "Limited" because they are not, cannot be, fully Jews, because there is a separation between their Jewish identity and their national identity or citizenship. Limited because they fulfill their state responsibilities, such as military service, as Americans or Frenchmen, rather than as Jews. In Israel, every facet of life is Jewish.

As a result of this approach, the Diaspora, on the other hand, is seen as lower on the scale of Jewish commitment. Even America—somehow recognized as better than other diasporas, since family and friends speak of it so often and so positively—even America is *Galut*—Exile. Exile is Pharaoh and Egypt. Slavery equals exile, not living in the Land of Israel. Freedom equals living in the Land. The Zionist thinker Ahad Haam, whose life bracketed the turn of this century, called the Zionist settlers and pioneers in the Land of Israel "the last generation of slavery, the first generation of freedom." The lesson is borne home during studies of the Holocaust, and is repeated again and again throughout Jewish history lessons, in Bible studies and in Hebrew literature.

All this is enhanced during military service, in youth movements, and in the high school para-military Gadna youth corps. On hiking tours and field trips, youngsters and soldiers are instilled with love of country as they are taught the history, geography and archeology of the area. One of the subjects taught is "battle heritage." Participants are told about the underground Zionist movements which were active during the British mandate, and the so called "illegal" immigration when the *Brichah* ("Flight"—to flee from Europe) organization moved tens of thousands of Jews across Europe and into Palestine. Mock "underground exercises" increase identification with national struggles of the past and with the generation of grandparents. Tracing the battles lines and supply routes of the War of Independence, the hikers cover the same hills and meet some of those who fought.

Israel's young are therefore enveloped in a set of attitudes and emotions prescribed by the realities of the present, the lessons of the past, holidays, music, songs, poetry and literature. The total effect is a Jew who is quite different from both Diaspora forebears and Diaspora relatives. The Bible is alive here. Its presence fills the imagination of Israeli children to such an extent that a constantly growing gap is created between Israeli "secular" Jews and non-Israeli Jews. This was brought home to an American poet some years ago by the following incident.

The six year-old girl, large-eyed and excited couldn't wait to tell her parents the news. This time she chose her father as the recipient. "Abba, guess who's pregnant?"

"How should I know? Tell me, who's pregnant?"

Triumphantly, the little girl said, "Sarah! Sarah's pregnant!"

The father, not really interested, "Who's Sarah? Which Sarah? Your teacher? The neighbor?"

The child: "Abba," a tone of disappointment and condescension in her small voice, "Abba, Sarah. Sarah, Avraham's wife. She's 90 and she's going to have a baby!"

The American poet, Stanley Burnshaw, was so moved by the story that he included it, in a slightly different version, in his long poem on Israel, *Mirages.** Ben Gurion, seemingly the pragmatist and rationalist, put this in mystical fashion, with the passion and true belief he had for the power of the Bible:

> Only to the people which settles anew in its Land and comingles with the landscape which shines forth from each page of the Book of Books—for whom the language of the Book becomes its natural language, in which it thinks and dreams— only to this people will the Book unfold the secret of its heart and its inner soul. The soul of the Book will become one with the soul of the people.

An all embracing life-style, Jewish in content and tone, makes Jewish life in Israel, *for all its secularity,* far more Jewish than it is in the Diaspora. In Israel the totality of the Jewish calendar establishes the rhythm of life for secular and religious alike. Every Jew in Israel is aware of the days which count: Sabbath and holidays. Voluntarily or not, to some extent everyone observes them regardless of individual

---

* Burnshaw, Stanley. *MIRAGES: Travel Notes in the Promised Land,* A Public Poem, New York, Doubleday & Co., 1977, p. 16.

religious beliefs; the law forbids or limits public transportation, closes all offices and factories except those with special permits, and maintains emergency services (police, fire and ambulances) at skeleton strength. Most restaurants are closed, almost all stores, food markets, and most cinemas as well. Admittedly, the essence of the day is different whether spent in synagogue or at the beach. An illustration of this is a Letter to the Editor from a kibbutz member:

> I, for one, observe the Sabbath in my own way, religiously. For me, it is a day entirely different from all the other days of the week—a day of rest and recreation, of different dress, a day with a special atmosphere: Sabbath, the Queen. The fact that I turn on the radio. . . or go to the beach with my family. . . makes it only more of a different day, more of a beloved Sabbath.
>
> That I do these things in Israel makes me more Jewish. . . than those Hasidim of my native Brooklyn who observe the Halachic Sabbath. That I served in the IDF [Israel Defence Forces] makes me more of a Maccabee than many of those. . . who keep the Sabbath rituals and shirk army service. . . . *

On Shabbat, as on holidays, the language changes. "Shalom" gives way to "Shabbat Shalom." Men and women bring flowers home on the eve of Sabbath and holidays. The pattern of traffic alters with nightfall on Friday, especially in Jerusalem. For some, Shabbat is not greatly different from a western Sunday, but for many, for most, it is a special day. Even in secular kibbutzim, there are vestigial candlesticks somewhere in the dining hall, tablecloths on the usually unadorned formica tabletops; throughout the country special Sabbath cultural events, public debates and "live interviews" are held. Radio and TV programming changes, reflecting the spiritual, cultural or recreational aspects of the day. Newspapers do not appear, leaving the Israeli soul more intact, uninvaded by the daily dose of the usually not very good news. The weekend paper comes out on Friday and it is richer, especially in cultural content

---

* *The Jerusalem Post*, January 3, 1988, Op-ed page. Reader's letter from Moshe Barzilai, Kibbutz Ein Hashofet.

(arts and literary section), but also in features and analysis than on other days.

Perhaps an obvious point. Ben Gurion spoke of the people dreaming in the language of the Bible. The radio, the lectures, almost all the cultural activities noted are in Hebrew. The obvious is often taken for granted. The Hebrew language was never simply one of prayer and learning; it was used in correspondence among Jews in many lands over long centuries. Hebrew was a major component of Yiddish and Ladino. Thus its revival as a living tongue of millions was easier, say than Gaelic in Ireland. Nonetheless its reemergence is unique. Isaiah or Jeremiah, our neighbors in Jerusalem, separated from us by millennia, speak to us. Their language is dated, ours slangy and sharp—and often sloppy. The accents are surely different. But the face is recognizable. The bone structure is unchanged.

The language has a soul which is associative. Even if the majority of people are not aware of all the associations, the literature and songs and children's nursery rhymes are infused with Bible and Mishnah and medieval poetic forms. Nobel Prize winner S.Y. Agnon's novels are an artful yet somehow natural fusion of Bible, Talmud, land and language. The most secular poetry in Israel often has Biblical cadences. The modern "Canaanite" poets, who would make Israelis into a modern Middle Eastern Semitic *but not Jewish* nation, with little or no contact with the rest of the Jewish people, write lines which breathe the Bible.

Our focus has been on living Zionism and Jewishness in Israel. Naturally, this is not a constant. We have been describing a model or "ideal" type which exists for large numbers and represents a majority consensus. But life, including that of a state and society, is dynamic. People change, history changes, and in Israel the social make-up and demography change rapidly.

CHANGES IN THE ISRAELI REALITY

Though Zionism, however defined, is the basis of Israel's national culture and civil religion, three far-reaching changes occurred in the social composition of the State and in its historic situation which have had a profound impact on Zionist ideology. These changes were in the demography of the Jews of Israel, in Israel as a pre-eminently Jewish state with a small Arab minority, and in the political climate and direction of the country from 1977 onward. In other words, we are dealing today with a different Jewish population in Israel, living in a changed internal political environment, and in a transformed relationship with the Arab (Palestinian) inhabitants of the State and of the occupied territories.

Demographically the Jewish "ethnic" mix moved from a predominantly *Ashkenazi* community to a land of *sabras*, with the majority either children of, or immigrants from the so-called Sephardi groups.* Nor is Israel any longer as pre-eminently Jewish in its composition. The number of Israeli Arabs has more than quadrupled since 1948 when the figure stood at 156,000. Furthermore, with the acquisition of the West Bank—Judea and Samaria—and Gaza in 1967, over a million additional Arabs came under Israeli control. Perhaps the most dramatic change occurred politically. In the elections of 1977, a labor-oriented secularist regime which had served for many years as the concrete and institutionalized expression of the civil religion and official Zionist ideology was ended overnight. It was replaced by a nationalist populist government established by the Likud, leaning increasingly on folk traditionalism and on small ultra-orthodox minority parties. The Likud has made Israel into a country in which Labor no longer automatically controls the levers of power. Labor fought hard in the early 1990s finally to regain precarious power.

A DIFFERENT PEOPLE

In 1948, Israel's Jewish population was 650,000; in the early 1990s, the Jewish population exceeded the 4,000,000 mark. Across the years, the composition of the population according to land of birth has changed dramatically.

Zionism's partially realized goal of ingathering the exiles changed Israel. European and Ashkenazi pioneers became the minority. Mass im-

---

* The term Sephardi is the adjective of *Sepharad*, Spain. Strictly speaking, many non-Ashkenazi Jews are not descended from the Sephardim, who were exiled from Spain and later Portugal some 500 years ago. For example, the Yemenite, Iraqi, Iranian and Georgian Jews among others, as well as the original Italian Jews of over two millennia ago all made their way into the Diaspora without passing through Spain.

migration to Israel in the first three-and-a-half years of statehood doubled the Jewish population. Displaced persons camps were emptied of Holocaust survivors. The Jews of Rumania and Yugoslavia came en masse. These were almost all Ashkenazi.

But the numbers of so-called and actual Sephardim swelled. The ancient communities of Iraq and Yemen and Bulgaria were all but completely uprooted as just about their entire Jewish population made their way to Israel. Morocco, Algeria and Tunis saw vast waves of emigrants set forth for the Promised Land. No wonder then that the present generation, the product of the immigration of the 1950s and 1960s, is overwhelmingly non-Ashkenazi.

The systematic annihilation of Jews by the Nazis in World War II destroyed the vast reservoir of potential immigrants from Europe. Many of these Jews were heir to a world outlook that was humanistic and secular. Others were in the process of secularizing. Either way they constituted an immense minority, if not an actual majority of European Jewry who rejected Halacha and rabbinic authority. Furthermore, those brought up in non-orthodox Zionist youth movements saw themselves, while yet in Europe, as patterned on the image of the "New Jew." In real life, this meant that they rejected Halachah and rabbinic authority.

Today, the less secularized lifestyle of the emigrants who came to Israel from Arabic-speaking lands, their ease with tradition and religious authority, is having great and growing impact on Israeli society. There appears to be a move back to a pre-modern combination of tradition and the acceptance of religious authority; an atmosphere decidedly less secular than during the hegemony of Eastern European Jewry. The "people base" for secularized Jewish settlement in Israel was wiped out by Hitler.

During the 50s and 60s, the Western model persisted in Israel and determined efforts were made to socialize and acculturate the immigrants from Arab and Islamic lands, the Sephardim, to the western mold. It was patronizing and it was condescending, but it was not conventional social snobbism. It was closer to the role played by American Jews from Germany and their later-arrived cousins, the "Americanized" Russian Jews who came in the 1880s to introduce the "greenhorns" of 1910 into American society. Yet the analogy is not completely apt, for underlying the Israel experience was a markedly different rationale. It was not merely that the Jews from Africa and Asia were seen as coming from backward or passive societies. There was also a sense of reviving Jewish history, of leaping from the degrading Galut to an historic new image of an entire people. This was not a case of acculturating to a "superior" America where the newcomers were simply an embarrassment and a potential "cause" of anti-Semitism.

The old-timers in Israel saw themselves as the "first generation of redemption," and they saw the newcomers as the "generation of the desert." It was a mix of Zionist passion and *Ahavat Yisrael,* true love of one's fellow Jew, and, condescension notwithstanding, offering the "best" values, the most "modern" ways which the old-timers treasured and wished to share with their "less-advanced" brothers. The fledgling citizens would now be molded into a new, much "better" form, an image fashioned on the myth of the pioneering years, of the kibbutz, of secularism, of the "New Jew." Some 20 years later, when latent resentment to all of this had built up to a point of explosion, the "patrons" were caught off guard, losing power for 17 years.

Consequently the children of new immigrants from the Arab countries inherited a mixed bag of myths. On the one hand, the image of the "New Jew"—strong, fearless, creating history, intrepid, resourceful, committed to social equality, in awe of physical labor, frowning on the "revealed" authority of religion, respecting those who wear the mantle of state authority and political leadership, ready to volunteer for tough pioneering civilian duty and dangerous military action.

And, alongside this, based on an opposing set of myths and a remembered grim reality, a second image: dispossessed new immigrants, deloused on arrival, housed in tent cities and tin-hut transit camps, children forced into orthodox and non-orthodox school systems according to a political party key rather than the parents' choice. And more memories, food rationing, public kitchens with strange Eastern European food, Ashkenazi food; sidelocks sometimes cut from pious little Yemenite boys; parents who had been petty merchants or *lumpenproletariat* suddenly working long hours in the sun, on relief projects and—perhaps most galling of all—told what to do by "disrespectful" younger men (and women!) ignorant of courtesy and politeness as "properly" practiced in the old country.

In this retrospective view of their absorption, the next stage is recalled as a continuation of the insult. It is the extended family, clustered around the grandparents, crowded into a tiny box-like flat in a shoddy housing project thrown up quickly, providing less than 500 square feet of living quarters for 6 to 10 people. Some families were doubled up in abandoned Arab housing. Still others were sent to farm villages and development towns, sometimes on unsettled frontiers, where they were taught self-defence and basic military skills.

They had grown up in a far-different world; the changes were overwhelming. From a society in which age was respected, they were brought to a place in which the older generation became the butt of jokes and a symbol of backwardness. Many could not cope. To be sure, in this description there is much romanticizing of the old country, since the process of urbanization and resultant crowded city life in all its ugliness and demeaning poverty had begun in North Africa and elsewhere.

But just as the Yiddish-speaking new immigrants to America glorified and romanticized the *shtetl,* so the Moroccan and Yemenite and Iraqi Jewish newcomers cast a haze of recalled tranquility and harmony and wholesomeness over their former lives. Again, not the reality of sociological studies, but the perceptions, the mythurgic longing for a Lost Paradise is what counts.

By the mid-70s, the right-wing populist *Likud* party (itself then led almost exclusively by Ashkenazim) had perfected its appeal to the dispossessed, and learned how to make room within its ranks for the rising generation of acculturated Sephardim. Labor stayed with the old-style ethnic bosses and power brokers. This was in part the background of the rise to power of the Likud in 1977. Internal developments in the Likud, however, in 1992 and later provided a setback for the outstanding example of the Sephardi banner-bearer, David Levy. Again, voices of his supporters could be heard castigating the "Ashkenazi bosses."

The ethnic component is only one element, however, not the whole story. The Yom Kippur War of 1973—Israel's lack of preparedness and the heavy casualties inflicted by Egypt and Syria—shattered public confidence in Labor. To a great extent, both factors, but, so it seems, particularly the injured pride of many Sephardim, also explains the subsequent rise of extremist and ethnic parties in the 1980s.

A word of caution and balance—for all the criticism and mistakes which marked the absorption process in the 50s and 60s, Israel did reach many of its goals. By and large, people were fed, housed, and educated. Probably it could have been done better, should have been done better, but given the constraints of budget and the dearth of experience, the achievement was simply that it was done. "Nobody," one prominent American Jew told me, "has written a 'do-it-yourself' book on how to build a state." And when the other odds are placed on the scale, the military threats and the political dilemmas faced by the young state, the story does take on the shimmering quality of a Biblical epic.

NEWER REALITY: RUSSIAN ALIYAH

The world turned topsy-turvy in the past few years: the first draft of this paragraph read: "It would seem that the USSR is in a stage of collapse." Now we see it has collapsed. Eastern Europe is seeking "democracy" and the material comforts of capitalist society. Chauvinism is now expressed openly under the new freedom; neo-fascistic influences appear which may be the fate and nemesis of the region.

Soviet policy-makers decided to let Soviet Jews emigrate. We must, for the purposes of this book, ignore the machinations within Jewish political leadership regarding where the "Russian" Jews should go, and the negligence of successive Israeli governments in preparing for the massive immigration. Small souls are usually present at miracles, and celebrate them after the fact. [For the sake of fairness, without the work of Israeli secret government bodies operating under cover in the former USSR, the groundwork for today's mass emigration would not have been laid.] The exodus of hundreds of thousands of Soviet Jews and their influx into Israel seems nothing less than miraculous. And so, thousands of ex-Soviet immigrants have poured into Israel. Of course, the economic breakdown of the communist system, and the revived anti-Semitism dormant in Russian soil and psyche are as powerful motivating factors as ideology—if not more so. Whatever the reasons, they come, and they will transform the face of Israel. The change will be qualitative as well as quantitative.

They will have an incalculable effect on Israel's Jewish soul. Few are learned Jewishly; most are totally ignorant of their religious, national or cultural heritage. They include highly sophisticated political operators, an unnatural proportion of university graduates (possibly one of every two newcomers, if initial reports are accurate) and men and women who learned to create and act with entrepreneurial initiative in a moribund economy. Many come with rich cultural assets: music, art, literature will feel their impact over the generations.

If the Jewish population swells to over four-and-a-half million over the next few years, the demographic imbalance with the Arab populace of Israel-Judea-Samaria will be less threatening.

History is the joker in the card deck of sociologists and political scientists. Again, a new Israel is being born. No one can predict its ultimate form and content.

A DIFFERENT COUNTRY

If the 1973 Yom Kippur War was a sobering and painful lesson for Israel, the 1967 Six-Day War was a revelation, and a revolution. At the end of May 1967, Israel saw itself as a tiny beleaguered nation. A week later Israelis became "like unto dreamers." Victory beyond all hopes had been achieved. Jerusalem reunited. The Land from the Mediterranean to the Jordan and Suez "conquered" or "liberated" and "redeemed." A decade earlier, in the headiness of the victory in the Sinai Campaign, even the usually sober Ben Gurion could speak of the "restoration of the Kingdom of David." Imagine then how Israelis felt on the morrow of the Six-Day War when, from real fear of destruction, Israel went on to push the Arab armies out of Sinai, all of the West Bank and the Golan heights.

"I am waiting for the phone call," Moshe Dayan said. The call from Cairo, or from Amman. The call which would say, "Let's talk peace." There was no phone call. There were messages, but they were conveyed by third parties and fourth parties, and there was yet another war to come. Ten years had to elapse before Saadat would come to Jerusalem.

In the meantime, another geographic, political and existential reality was evolving. Since that June day in 1967, Israel controls and administers territories inhabited by Arabs, mostly Moslem, in what is called the West Bank (Judea and Samaria) and in the Gaza area. All told, some one-and-a-quarter million Arabs, who speak their own language and whose earth revolves around an entirely separate cultural and religious axis, now live under Israeli rule. (The peace negotiations, underway as I write, may succeed. If they do, the changes effected until

1993 on Israeli reality and perception will nonetheless remain an indivisible part of Israel's psyche, politics and society.)

One may certainly argue that after the dizzying victory in the Six-Day War of 1967, Israel had no choice but to maintain control over these territories: that there was no Arab partner with whom to negotiate their disposition. One may also argue that as occupations go, the Israeli record—even with undeniable lapses—has been a "benign" one. The political implications and the moral wisdom of the issue will provide grist for the mills of historians and political scientists for decades.

One may argue just the opposite: that Israel could have withdrawn totally or in part from the territories, or have walked away—even unilaterally—from Gaza, for example, or introduced local or regional autonomy, and so on. No doubt political leadership in Israel has not overwhelmingly convinced and carried the Israeli people nor its supporters abroad of its policies. The country is divided, and often confused. Only one Israeli leader, Ben Gurion, could possibly have led Israel away from its dizzying victory—but his time was past. Labor ambivalence and Likud ideology led to a growing Israeli presence in the areas of Judea, Samaria and Gaza. Religious drives and nationalist compulsions held much of the Israeli public in their thrall.

Ultimately, Israelis deal with realities and perceptions: forms and shadows; the shadow of fear of being swamped by Arabs, versus the shadow of fear that we are losing our own selves and identity in a political and military morass which is insoluble. The mixture of history and religion, new-found power and ethnic hostility, *hutzpa* and *hubris*, righteousness and self-righteousness is dizzying, yet choices must be made. The demographic swing has strengthened the right wing. Politicians of both left and right, as well as in the more extreme ultra-orthodox-cum-ethnic parties have played to the hilt the "ethnic" (*edah*: origin group) question. It is not one of Israel's proud moments, and some politicians have cynically played the role of spokesmen for the "downtrodden." In exploiting the "exploited," they have made it into quite a good thing.

(That is not to say that Arab leadership has provided foresight and vision. The cynicism of both Palestinian and Arab state leaders since 1948 is a fit subject for study, though obviously not here. From the Arab perspective, the intifada must be seen as a "victory." That it has exacted not only hundreds of Jewish casualties, but thousands of Arab killed and wounded, will only add to the National Myth of the Palestinians. In writing their history, they will forget that more Arabs were killed by Arabs than by Israelis, or that the PLO and other terrorist leaders lived abroad on large bank-accounts while calling for "steadfastness" from their poorer and unhappy compatriots at home. The perception of the Arabs must be taken into account, just as we do in this book for Jewish perceptions.)

To return to our subject, most Israelis, however divided they may be on the future of these territories, know that Arabs prefer Arab rule to Israeli occupation. Most Israelis acknowledge as well that holding these territories imposes grave burdens on the Israeli army and the security forces. A great many Israelis, not all of the left, are afraid that occupation warps our society and economy, our politics and our social mores, our inner core of morality. Pending another solution, under international conventions Israel is responsible for maintaining law and order and guaranteeing fair conditions of life.

Thousands of Israeli soldiers are deployed in the territories to maintain control. The soldiers range in age from 18-year-olds on their regular three-year tour of duty to reservists in their 40s. Their tasks range from the civilian aspects of military government which affect the day-to-day life of the Arab population, health, work permits, travel, financial and economic matters, to crowd and riot control, patrols searching for anti-Israeli groups, pursuing terrorists, and seeking out those who throw rocks or petrol bombs at passing traffic. That is, simply stated, meeting violence with violence.

In other words, though some soldiers and civilian employees of the military government deal with the Arab population with the intent of making life as "normal" as possible, others are engaged in confrontations which include the use of force. These mostly very young men and women (boys and girls?) perform an unpleasant and often dangerous service. They are ordinary people, husbands and wives, sons and daughters.

These exigencies and political realities are at one level of national life. They are a constant and nagging subliminal echo of political dissension and endless debate over Israel's policies toward an eventual solution. On another level, debate involves the psychological and moral implications. On this issue, even in the peace negotiations of 1992 and 1993, a national consensus does not exist. In 1967, most Israelis were electrified to see that the previous borders which had defined Israel from 1948 to 1967 seemed to have "run away" miles eastward. This revived the sense that the land is one, and that the previous frontiers were artificial. An important segment of the population believes that this is God-given and pre-ordained.

Most Israelis are concerned that Israel's pre-1967 frontiers were too fragile, that the narrow waistline of that Israel, barely 10 miles wide between the Arab towns and villages in the foothills and Netanya on the Mediterranean was a permanent invitation to cut the tiny country in half. (Pre-1967 Israel was about 8,000 square miles in area, and even today with the occupied areas it is only some 10,000 square miles.) Therefore it seems clear that a majority of Israelis would not agree to an Arab state which could deploy military forces on the western (Israel) side of the Jordan River.

In 1968, while the territories were calm, while stunned Arabs strove to recover from the total collapse of their leadership in the face of the devastating Israeli victory, it may well have been relatively easy to annex the territories. Indeed there were a few Israelis (they were still a small minority) who counseled just such a course of action. Prime Minister Levi Eshkol, a bear of a man who wore a peasant-like cloak of folk wisdom about himself, responded characteristically, "What can we do? We like the dowry, but not the bride." Certainly today the bride is an unwilling one. The dowry—the territories—are an indistinguishable part of the same geographic region, a region so small that on a map the word ISRAEL must be printed on the adjoining blue of the Mediterranean.

The longer the present situation continues, the closer grow the ties between Arabs who are citizens of Israel and those who live under Israeli administration but are not citizens of Israel. Citizenship is one thing; national identity, nationalist sympathies and mobilization are another. The widespread demonstrations and riots, the *intifada*, which began in December 1987 were not confined to Judea, Samaria or Gaza. They spilled over into a number of Israeli Arab towns and centers like Nazareth and Jaffa where, even if violence did not burst forth as strongly, Arab feelings of solidarity run high.

Demonstrations and tensions are not the only signs of frustrated Arab nationalism. Throughout the entire Middle East—actually it might be more exact to say throughout the entire world—religious fundamentalism is on the ascent. Iran is dramatic evidence of this. Moslem fundamentalism is rising in a tidal wave which washes across borders and countries with increasing impetus.

THE INTIFADA: AN IRREVERSIBLE CHANGE?

As this is being written, the intifada has been going on for over six years. The Middle East is unpredictable. The Iraqi invasion of Kuwait is just one example. And the Palestinian reaction, inviting Iraq to gas Israeli cities, with wild demonstrations of truly deep-seated hatred has forced Israelis of all opinions to reconsider the possibility of peaceful coexistence with their Arab neighbors within "Greater Israel."

At any rate, it seems today that the intifada has wrought an irreversible change in Israel, and in Israel-Arab relations. It probably has had the same effect on Israel's friends in foreign governments, as well as on the Jewish people. The intifada may lead to peace and peace to reconciliation. Who can do more than hope?

The spectrum of response to the problem of the Jewish-Arab demographic balance in the greater Land of Israel is wide. There are the out-and-out annexationists, some of whom are ready to pay Arabs to leave, or to arrange a "transfer" of populations. To help the departure along, some would make the life of the Arab civil population within the territories unbearable. There are others who regretfully accept the fact that the Arabs have a right to remain where they are, or that world opinion requires that they be permitted to remain, but who believe that "massive" settlement by Jews should have as its aim the containment of Arabs within the villages or towns in which they live today, while all available State land should be settled by Jews. Others seek peace, a return of part of the territories, and pacts of neighborliness and understanding.

There are those who feel that the occupation has already taken its toll on Israeli morality. The debate is so charged, the schism so profound, that the seeds of Jewish internal strife seem to some to have already taken root. The whirlwind of bloodshed bordering on actual civil strife, however brief, may yet blow across the land.

For good reason was the Six-Day War called the Cursed Blessing. The Romans, military power holders of their era, said: *Vae victoribus, vae victis!* Woe unto the victors, woe unto the vanquished!

A generation of Jews has grown up in direct personal and often physical confrontation with a generation of Arabs who have learned to hate even more deeply. Hate engenders hate. In 1967, Israelis could say, "We do not hate the Arabs."

Thus, since 1967 everything has changed—the people, the land, the outlook for peace, the moral dilemmas—and therefore the ideology. The prototype of the "New Jew" who reflected the realities of European Jewry and early Zionism is not dead, it lingers on in the national psyche. But other prototypes compete with it, an expression of a new way of thinking, of an ideology which flows out of a new reality.

CHAPTER FIVE

THE NEW ISRAEL: A PARTIAL SUMMARY

The earlier chapters of this book dealt with the non-orthodox Israeli, the "New Jew," and the changes reality has wrought in this prototype. The newer picture of the Israeli is different: the majority of Israel's Jewish population today is more traditional and conservative in its life style.

How is this reality reflected in the way people live and express their Jewishness? What is the rhythm of life? How do tradition and *halachah* affect Israeli Jewish life? In other words, what elements of the halachah are observed by the people today? How do Israelis view themselves and the Diaspora? First, what do people observe in close or complete conformity with the halachah?

Most religions have specific rituals for the rites of passage, for birth, maturation, marriage, death. Judaism, as with some other religions, also has a code of forbidden and permitted foods—*kashrut.* Taking the observance of these rituals as indicators, polls show that close to half the Jews in Israel observe a basic form of kashrut. We can assume that even more practice some elements of kashrut's food taboos. Similarly, a majority follow rabbinical procedure:

> in the case of circumcision (overwhelmingly if not totally observed);
> in celebrating the bar-mitzvah passage of boys into pre-adulthood (widely observed, including the synagogue service in which the celebrant is called to the Torah for the first time);
> in registering for marriage and in conducting the wedding ceremony and for dissolving marriage (divorce);
> in funeral arrangements and burial services.

However, the sway of the orthodox rabbinate over marriage and death is not as widely accepted and has led to bitterness and "consumer resistance." In both cases, the forbidding and medieval mien of many of the officials responsible has brought families to feel that the power of the rabbinate is too all-embracing. Obtrusive questions about the observance of ritual purity offend many young women and their families.*

Anger and resentment at the rabbinate is not limited to civil libertarians who, as a matter of principle, oppose the monopoly of the rabbinate over the rites of passage. For many young people who are not familiar with the tradition and have no contact with rabbis except on such occasions, the customs surrounding these rites are beyond their experience. This creates further alienation from, or actual animosity towards orthodoxy. In part, the rabbinate in Israel is to blame for this, in that the rabbis are chosen for Talmudic learning only, without concern for university education or special training for a pastoral role. Nonetheless, a majority probably turn willingly, or at least with acceptance to the rabbinate for these essential services.

The late Yigal Allon, a national leader widely respected in Israel, once said that though he was from the political Left, he would wish his children to be married in the traditional way. Otherwise, Allon, a Labor leader and kibbutznik, feared that observant Jews would cease to marry non-observant Jews, creating an irreparable rift within the Jewish people.

In dealing with death, the role of the orthodox burial society is to carry out rabbinic injunctions rather than to offer comfort to the family. Under the best of circumstances funerals are traumatic. A family totally removed or far distant from religion, is bound to have great difficulty in facing the stark burial ceremony. The body is not encased in a coffin but is interred in a plain cloth shroud. The male survivors must recite prayers which they may never have seen before, and the closest kin have a cut or rip made in their shirt or blouse as a sign of separation and mourning.

Some non-religious people take comfort in this simplicity, others

---

* Married women are required to observe separation from sexual or other contact with their husbands during and following their menses. Then a "ritual bathing" (*mikveh*) ceremony is performed, after which the couple returns to its normal sex life. Brides are required to immerse themselves in the mikveh prior to the marriage ceremony.

vociferously object to it or accept it with silent resentment. What is surprising is to see that, outside the kibbutz, many families observe the *shiv'ah*, the seven-day mourning period, often with daily prayers in the home. Many male mourners do not shave during that week, sometimes for the entire 30 days (*shloshim*) after the funeral. Perhaps it is natural for people to search for comfort in continuity and structure at a time of loss.

Despite these criticisms of religious observance, the majority of the Jewish population in Israel classifies itself as traditional. This may include, in addition to the laws of *kashrut*, the rites described above; some measure of Sabbath and holiday family ceremonials, or sometime attendance at synagogue services. Since the numbers of the fully orthodox have increased, more non-practicing Jews attend ceremonies of their orthodox relatives. To some extent, on such occasions, lines may be blurred.

In short, the life style has become more traditional. And the more traditional it becomes, the more threatened become those elements of the population who are consciously or ideologically secular. They are on the defensive. This perception of being under attack, of being spiritually beleaguered flourishes against the backdrop of the political system which enhances the power of smaller parties.

SABBATH IN JERUSALEM

Shabbat, the day of peace and spiritual restoration has on occasion become a political football. The two angels of peace which in tradition escort Jews home from synagogue Friday evening after prayers are often dragged to demonstrations outside a cafe or movie theater. Sometimes traffic is stoned on roads near ultra-orthodox neighborhoods. Anti-orthodox young people organize their own demonstrations and counter-demonstrations. More stones are thrown. The police intervene, mounted charges break up the demonstrations. Neither side is happy. . . .

"Nazis!" The pious call the policemen, themselves mostly traditional Jews forced to leave their families and Sabbath tables to "keep the peace." It is a heartbreaking picture made worse because the principles of the sanctity of the Sabbath and of Jerusalem are in conflict with the principles of individual freedom and the right to exercise an individual lifestyle. It is the Jewish fascination with Divine Will on the one hand,

and democratic human values on the other. Without this two-edged fanaticism, would we be what we are? With it, can we coexist? Can we live together in respect and tolerance?

There is the other deep schism which cuts across society and families: the future of Israel and the occupied territories. To which must be added questions of God's will and secular nationalism, historic ties to the land and political expediency, the Holocaust syndrome and Moslem fundamentalism. It is a melange of unstable elements. The footsteps of Messiah. The birthpangs of a new period. All being inscribed on a grim and glorious historical scroll. All involving life-and-death decisions. Not just for Israelis, but for all Jews. And not just for Jews alone.

These are some of the newer realities. A new Jewish people is being formed in its homeland, facing existential situations which Jews in the Diaspora need not face. Here the people is growing in a pervasiveness Jewish atmosphere, rhythms of public and family life, education and culture. At the same time, it is a people confronting strife as the walls of consensus are stretched by conflict, hopefully to give birth to a new *modus vivendi*, to a new consensus. This modus vivendi will need to embrace the two most burning issues wrenching Israeli society today: the role of religion in day-to-day life, and the future of Israel and the territories of Judea, Samaria and Gaza.

*ATTITUDES TOWARD THE DIASPORA**

If the rebirth of Israel, with all its failings, is a great historic adventure, why do so many Israelis forsake Israel for other havens? Why are there so many ex-Israelis "temporarily" or not-so-temporarily living in Los Angeles and New York and Toronto. . . . in tens of cities ranging from Johannesburg to Berlin? If Israelis are indeed taught to negate the Diaspora, and if they are indeed living through such an unparalleled saga, one which teaches them that they cannot and should not live in the Diaspora, how is it that hundreds of thousands of Israelis have left Israel for the Diaspora? And why do Israelis who stay at home so eagerly emulate American styles and fads in their lifestyle? Are they trying to create a Hebrew-speaking America in Israel? When American Jews ac-

---

* For further discussion, see Section Two on American Jewry.

cuse Israelis of "materialism," is the pot calling the kettle black, or is Israel indeed just another westernized materialistic society? Where is the "New Jew?" Where is the dream?

There are the usual explanations. Some real, some sociological theories or pseudo-history, some in the vague realms of social psychology or political science that deal with "national character." For example, all lands of immigration have unhappy immigrants who return home. . . . Jews have more possibilities of emigration because they have relatives in many countries. . . . Jews are a wandering folk and have no tradition of rootedness. . . . *Ubi bene, ibi patria* —where it is good, there is my homeland. . . . Some Israelis are tired of war. . . . Some Israelis put their profession before patriotism. . . . Israel's economic potential militates against making money. . . . The political and economic system makes it hard to be an entrepreneur. . . . Taxation is too high. . . . and so on. And quite likely many of these points are true or partly true.

But there are factors which go beyond these. And since they are iconoclastic, they are often disavowed, swept under the carpet by apologists in Israel and abroad. As Israel strives to form a national culture in which at least its Jewish citizens feel fully at home, underlying it all is a spiritual and cultural malaise. Israel's culture is remarkably rich and varied (particularly for a country with such a small population) whether measured in book titles published per year (over 5,000);

> in symphony orchestras and smaller classical ensembles which abound in city and town;
> in the seven institutes of higher learning with 50,000 students at all levels;
> in the number of Torah institutes, also with some 50,000 students;
> in the rich literature of the Hebrew language in all fields of *belles lettres*;
> in children's literature which seems as natural and rooted as Mother Goose.

Yet. . . yet the prevailing popular culture is typical of a country which is unsure of its identity. This is a problem which is common to societies which undergo rapid and dramatic changes such as urbanization, industrialization, or mass immigration. The problem is compounded when these transitions occur in an era of mass culture which invades all corners of life as a result of the communications revolution.

In country after country we have now seen society undergo immense changes—revolutions in lifestyle—over the last century. Massive internal migrations moved people from the simple life to a more complicated existence in large cities with great industrial centers. Emigration cast millions from country to country, precipitating a crisis in identity and home values. The traditional yields to the modern. In Israel, all these processes have occurred in a whirlwind, like a movie film being run at double or triple speed.

The uprooted groups came trooping home, crossing oceans of time and space. Mass immigration. A new (old-new but new) language. Other values. Other mores. Always other. While those who have lived in Israel—say seventy years, or fifty, or twenty years remained in the same place. But the place changed beyond recognition under their very feet. In a sense they too are displaced people, whose "place" is the same and yet not at all what it was.

In this upheaval, as traditional values give way, the West and especially America seem to offer new sureties: glamour, comfort, efficiency, progress, technology, in short, all the good things in the world are made in America. Arnold Toynbee, the historian, described the process of "westernization" in the misleadingly simple phrase, "One thing leads to another."* If U.S. technology is desirable, can its lifestyle be far behind? Missiles and advanced military hardware bring American mass culture in their wake. If you want F-16s, you also get Coca-Cola. In Israel, with Coca-Cola, we have received some of the most vulgar and least valuable elements of popular American/western culture.

After World War II, America's immense influence on Western Europe and Asia caused the process of modernization to spread even more quickly, borne not only on the wings of military and political alliances, but also on infusions of capital and transfers of know-how through the Marshall plan, investments and economic aid.

In Palestine, the British were the people in charge, under a League

---

* Arnold Toynbee, *The World and the West* (London: Oxford University Press, 1953). The term "westernization" smacks of imperialism nowadays, and has been replaced by the more neutral "modernization."

of Nations mandate (which followed their victory over the Turks) from December, 1917 until May 1948.* The English language and customs became a norm which the "natives"—even when rebelling against Britain—adopted. It is not an unusual phenomenon in colonial rule. Britain's mantle as the center of gravity and power in the West, and more specifically as the most significant economic and political factor for Israel and the Middle East was inherited by the United States, the predisposition to see English as the language of progress was transferred to the American idiom.

Nor was it the sophistication of language alone which had to be emulated, but the culture which that language bore. This process occurred as the burgeoning media made it possible for America to move mass culture into every home. American popular music, American television programs, American styles of radio broadcasting and television production were omnipresent, hitting an audience to some extent already culturally deracinated and struggling to redefine its identity.

A curriculum vitae of the Israeli population must include the upheavals which traversed Europe in this century and then spread to the Mediterranean basin, Asia and Africa; the Bolshevik Revolution, Nazism and the Holocaust; and the Israeli wars described earlier. To all of these must further be added the basic religious and cultural conflicts within Israel and the political schism over the question of the territories. Thus we are dealing with a people whose identity has gone through immense changes, upheavals and internal tensions.

There are a number of elites capable of defining their identity in cultural terms or at least willing to struggle to define it. A larger part of the population settles for the mass ("Americanized") culture which forms its adoptive identity. It is this mass culture which tends to make some Israelis seem—superficially—to be Hebrew-speaking "Americans."

The term elite is misleading since not every elite is a cultural elite. For example, not all of Israel's "technological" elite is able to define itself as separate from this mass culture. On the contrary, sometimes, the more its members relate to American technology, the more prone they are to define themselves primarily as technologists. . . . And then the

---

* The Mandate was actually confirmed by the Council of the League of Nations on July 24, 1922. Until then the British ruled by right of conquest.

decision to get the technology first-hand, and work in the U.S. may not be so far behind, while salary considerations, though not primary, may well be of equal importance.

Studies on *yeridah* also show—not surprisingly—that the lower the level of Jewish identity, the higher the possibility of leaving Israel.* (*Yeridah* is the opposite of *aliyah*. In the context of Jews coming to live in Israel, *aliyah* means to go up—physically and spiritually—to Zion; *yeridah* means to descend, to go down, and carries with it a negative sense of desertion.)

Israel society has been presented with a double message: 1) Zionism and Israel are "best"—Israel is the only place in which a Jew can feel free, redeemed, creative as a Jew; 2) America is "best"—American know-how, capital, wealth, lifestyle are all to be emulated if one wishes to "succeed," be up-to-date, live well, make money.

This double message came through early in statehood as Israelis experienced a deep ambivalence toward fundraising efforts on behalf of Israel. In those early years the absolute dependence of Israel on these campaigns was widely recognized. At the same time, many Israelis openly—and almost all in the disquiet of their hearts—resented the dependence. This created a tension which appeared to be alleviated by poking fun at a stereotyped "contributor"—Bermuda shorts, Hawaiian shirt, camera hanging down over a protruding belly, large cigar, and yachting cap or baseball hat, visiting Israel to see his "project" or his "boys."

Today the double message troubles those dealing with fundraising for Israeli institutions, who themselves unconsciously foster an "America-is-best" attitude. Imagine the following scene: The auditorium in "Kiryat Ma-Shehu" is festooned with flags and bunting. Present are a cabinet minister, the mayor and the head of the residents' committee or hospital or school—as the case may be. Excited children who have been drilled for days file in, sing and dance. Speeches praising the contributor follow. The children return home excited, impressed. They mention vast sums contributed, and how everyone wished to please the donors. The message they have received is that indeed it is more blessed to give than to receive! So why not live where the blessed live?

---

* See Simon Herman, *Israelis and Jews*, New York, Random House, 1970. Chap. 4.

The image of the individual donor as an American has been enhanced by the vast infusions of capital coming from the United States. Beginning with a hundred-million dollar loan from the Export-Import Bank under the Truman administration in 1949, through to Point Four technological aid during the crucial 1950's, and ending with yesterday's loan or grant or arms purchases from the U.S., American power and wealth have become part and parcel of Israel's economic and military viability. America then is the lodestone of power, success and modernity.

But the very attraction to America creates resentment. And the power and influence of American Jewry, though respected and appreciated, spur a perverse ambivalence, that of the weak toward the strong who help them. In a way, it is the "poor relative" syndrome. "Poor but proud." *All they have is money. We have values. They write checks. We give blood.* Which Israeli has not had such thoughts steal through his mind?

The old ghost of "Galut-Jew" breaks out of its shrouds: the Jew in Exile, who, so the stereotype would claim, does not have the pride to stand up for Israel when it is not popular to do so. *The inequality of risk.* Is the blood of my children purer than that of yours? You take pride in our victories? Money and political support are easy. It makes you feel virtuous and a "good Jew." What right do you have to judge? Ultimately, if you are not ready to join us here, you are betraying Jewish history.

For most Israelis perhaps it is this last point which counts. "Love of Israel" is one thing; sharing Israel's life and joys, troubles and struggles is another. For some, it may be simply old-fashioned jealousy and resentment. For others, it is more abstract, perhaps the knowledge that Israel had to be built by those who came, while those who "stayed" were far better equipped educationally and financially to make the task of building easier. It may be the sense that history was waiting for all the Jews to recognize the great historical moment. Yet they voted with their feet and their pocketbooks to stay in Egypt, and Moses had to cross the Red Sea and Joshua enter the Promised Land with "the generation of the desert." The Diaspora then is envied and resented, castigated and emulated. It attracts Israelis almost "fatally," while it angers and repels them partly because of that very attraction.

Yet. . . . Snatches of conversation at army bases along the Lebanese border, in the Golan, and in a tent in Lebanon itself, the year after the "Peace in Galilee" war: We're fighting for "them" as well. If Jews are attacked anywhere, we have to defend them. . . . If terrorists can kill Israelis, they'll kill Jews in the Galut that much more easily. . . . Who needs them? If they don't want to live here, we don't want their money either. . . . Come on, we couldn't last without them. . . . What are you talking about? All they raise is two percent of our GNP!. . . . Okay, but what about the political help and the money the U.S. government sends because of their work. . . . Sure, but if they were here, we'd be so big and competent, we'd manage better!. . . . Maybe we should work to keep them close to us and then maybe more will want to come. . . . Maybe. . . .

The ideology internalized. Ordinary people trying to understand themselves, their condition, and their place in Jewish history. Did Jews returning from Babylon over two-and-a-half millennia ago hold the same discussions? Was this the debate in Jerusalem two thousand years ago during the Second Commonwealth? Will these debates be studied one day as a political Jerusalem Talmud of the twentieth century?

Today's debate penetrates every level of Israeli society, whether in the measured tones of academics, the impassioned cadences of ideologues, the hectored point-scoring of politicians, or the *ex cathedra* exchanges among shoppers in the *shuk*! When there is such an ongoing debate over the Jewish condition and the meaning of Jewish history, is this not in itself a powerful expression of the centrality of Jewishness and ideology in Israel's life?

Against this general background, Israel continues its natural development as an independent culture: Hebraic, national, a state utilizing instruments of power. The Diaspora too holds to its course as a minority, non-Hebraic, and using instruments of influence in a non-Jewish milieu. The trends are contradictory, leading inevitably to distancing. Criticism of Israel's religio-political system and of its political stance accelerates this historic evolution.

The dangers of political estrangement between Israel and the Diaspora are so great for all concerned that one may assume that they will be avoided or downplayed. In spite of the strains, both sides still share basic loyalties to continued Jewish existence, and for all the distance, mutual concerns seem—meanwhile—to outweigh clashes of interest and style. In the short run. The real danger is the much deeper one of cultural estrangement, the inability of the younger generations in both communities to share their worlds of experience and universes of discourse.

Israeli culture and peoplehood are still being shaped. The State is in existence for two generations, some 40 years, and has yet to traverse the extreme civil strains on its sovereignty which almost every modern Western state has experienced in cementing its unity and peoplehood. The great countries of migration such as the United States, Canada and Australia required a century or a century-and-a-half to fashion their identity, political independence and unity. It took that long, if not longer, to create a free-standing and authentic national culture.

The speed of modern communication may exert an influence on the time that is needed for Israel to shape its full identity and cultural personality. Modernity, though, has not been able to change the time needed for plants and animals to reach maturity. We can assume the same holds true of a nation's body politic and of its soul, the national culture.

As internal and external problems mount, Israel will undoubtedly enter a period of greater soul-searching and disillusion. This period of the State's adolescence—if Israel's saga unfolds in line with that of other new nations—will be outgrown, but not without severe crisis, and possibly civil strife. The stage of critical mass has been passed, but the more profound Israel's message is to its own citizens and to their fellow Jews, the more exhilarating will be its present stage of searching and experimentation. As Israel achieves increasing cultural maturity, their path will continue to diverge further and further from that of Diaspora Jewry.

CHAPTER SIX

AMERICA'S JEWS: LIFESTYLE AND IDEOLOGY

Is the American Jewish community en route to becoming a separate people in its own right?

The ties which held together the brothers of three or four generations ago—common roots, similar religious patterns or ideological adherence, shared language, and loyalty to the Jewish calendar—these ties are attenuated, frayed. If Israeli Jews see themselves as having cast off the Diaspora experience and creating a new Jewish/Hebrew society and culture, American Jews tread a completely different path.

First and foremost, American Jews see themselves as American. They do not believe that they are in Exile. They believe they are part of an overall American reality based on equality of citizenship, full civil rights, and active involvement in the economic, political and academic life of the country.

To an Israeli, what is most astonishing is the clear-cut American identity of his cousins. For example, during the early years of Israel's statehood, in conversations with "average" Jews who were committed to Israel, one heard statements like the following which demonstrate the rootedness of American Jews in American history. "Our forefathers came to this country and had to fight the British for their independence, so we can identify with Israel because Israel had to fight them too."

In fact, his forefathers did not come sailing to America's wooded shores on the Mayflower; the likelihood is that they escaped the Czarist military draft only a few generations earlier. But identification with America is total—with America and American history. And this negates the perception that American Jews live in Exile. On the contrary, the civil religion of American Jews reverses some basic Jewish symbols in order to invest Americanism with the cachet or "kashrut-label" of Judaism.

In the United States, the Jews have made and continue to make every effort to "Judaize" the symbols of Americanism, that is to bring the American civil religion into harmony with their own Jewish religious and historical symbols. Their task is made easier by the fact that the Bible-loving Puritan founding fathers fleeing religious persecution saw America as the new Zion.

AMERICA: THE NEW PROMISED LAND

The Jewish Theological Seminary of America (JTS) is the training ground for spiritual leaders and teachers of Conservative Judaism. A report in one its publications, "Sinai and the Constitution" illustrates the merging of the symbols of American civil religion and those of Judaism.

> The Seminary, as one of the major faith groups funded by the National Broadcasting Company to produce a TV special on The Promise of America, debated for weeks on an appropriate subject, finally settling on the United States Constitution. . . . The documentary compares two covenants, that of Sinai and the Constitution. . . .

Sinai is the Covenant between the Jewish people and God. Just as Sinai is the overwhelming historic event of Jewish peoplehood, the cornerstone of its religion, so too the American Constitution is embraced by the civil and religious symbolism of American Judaism. The message is that God gave the Torah at Sinai and the American Constitution at Philadelphia. Two "equal" covenants.

Another instance. In 1981, the Jewish establishment in San Francisco produced a film on its community for screening at an international reunion of major Jewish benefactors. The documentary bore the title, "San Francisco: Jerusalem by the Golden Gate!"

Using Judaic symbols, American Jews as a matter of course, almost off-handedly sanctify America until it indeed becomes a new Zion. The JTS documentary, according to its report, "shows the extent to which the early colonists identified with the ancient Israelites, seeing themselves as redeemed . . . . speaking in such Biblical metaphors as the promised land. . . . "

The promised land. Jerusalem by the Golden Gate. Sinai, the Covenant with God, and the U.S. Constitution—two covenants. The "parallels between halachah" and the Constitution. Three basic symbols of Judaism: The Sinaitic Covenant (the giving of the Torah and the revelation of God); the halachah which is based on Torah and Talmud and an unbroken line of rabbinical authorities; and Jerusalem, Zion, the Promised Land.

These film documentaries say more about the perception of Judaism and Jewishness by Jews in America than statements of Jewry's theological and community leaders. Reality is the way people live and see themselves. And this means that the folk religion, the civil religion of American Jews is Americanism. In American Jewish homes, as in most modern Western homes, the power of film and television is more pervasive than Hebrew or a residual Jewish heritage. It enters the living room or den or bedroom with intimacy and enormous impact.

AMERICA IS NOT EXILE

This positive strengthening of the Americanism of U.S. Jews with the use of ancient Jewish symbols is matched by a negative approach to the notion of Exile, *Galut*. Jews simply feel at home in America; at least most Jews feel at home in America most of the time.

At a fundraising meeting in a small New England town some years ago, a woman asked the speaker if, when the Messiah came she "would have to" go to Israel. He replied that those Jews who believed in a personal Messiah also believed that he would lead them to the Land of Israel. She blurted out, almost in tears: *"But I don't want to go to Israel! I was born here. My parents were born here. They're all buried here. I don't want to have to go to Israel."*

The secular or civil religion of American Jews rests on a single foundation: American Jews are American. Their Judaism must fit the American ideology and culture. Their strivings and their religious behavior must relate to the American context. For them, the term Galut is irrelevant. As a religious and ethnic minority, their ties to the past and their links in the present with Jews overseas and with Israel—the Land, State and people—must all be viewed through American lenses.

65

THE AMERICAN JEWISH CIVIL RELIGION

A richly documented study suggests that American "civil" Judaism affirms seven major tenets, which together "define the American Jewish civil religion's essential world view and ethos:"*

1. The unity of the Jewish people
2. Mutual responsibility
3. Jewish survival in a threatening world
4. The centrality of the State of Israel
5. The enduring value of Jewish tradition
6. Tzedakah: philanthropy and social justice
7. Americanness as a virtue.

The author did not find it necessary to state the obvious: that American Jewry wished to remain in America, and that America was not *Galut.*

But principles do not really indicate how people live. Neither do they describe the cultural atmosphere of the American Jew. How he lives indicate what he believes: his life and existential experience shape his way of seeing the world. What makes up the rhythm of his life, the inner calendar of the mundane, as well as the pace of his days of hope and memory?

THE HOLIDAYS AND HOLY DAYS OF AMERICAN JEWS

The days which American Jews observe in their overall (that is, American) civil religion are the national holidays of the Fourth of July—U.S. Independence Day, and Thanksgiving. But Christian holidays proper are also part of the reality of American Jewish life. This is true, notwithstanding the official separation of Church and State, since the tenor of American life is Christian.

The rhythm of life in the United States resonates to the key holy days of the Christian calendar, alongside those of the American civil religion. Thus Christmas and Easter, New Year's Day, the Fourth of July and Thanksgiving Day form the pillars of the year. True the purely Christian side of the first two undergo metamorphoses in consciously

---

* Jonathan S. Woocher, *Sacred Survival, The Civil Religion of American Jews,* Bloomington and Indianapolis, Indiana University Press, 1986, pp. 67-68.

Jewish homes, while New Year's is basically a secular holiday. But their dominance is pervasive, and sets the calendar for American Jewry, with isolated (and sometimes insular) exceptions, such as the hasidic and *yeshiva* islands in New York and New Jersey.

Thanksgiving has become a holiday for all Americans, and Jews have sought specific ways of marking it within a Jewish context, for example in the synagogue service on the preceding Sabbath. Since it is a family holiday which the extended circle celebrates at a festive dinner, it fits nicely into the Jewish religious familial pattern. The Thanksgiving theme, escape from religious oppression in the Old World to freedom in the New, continues the Exodus motif, a perfect example of the naturalization of Judaism in America.

Christmas and Easter have an integral role in the work and school cycle of the United States (as in most countries in Europe and the Americas) since they are both religious and civil statutory holidays. School break and vacation or holiday time set the rhythm of society. Christmas especially, which has been adopted by retailers and merchandisers as a great sales promotion opportunity, becomes the constant theme of television, radio, the press and of casual conversation.

One would think that the secularization and commercialization of Christmas has made it a holiday more "American civic" than Christian in some senses. Yet Jews have felt so pressed by the underlying content that a number of surrogates have been invented. For example, in areas of large Jewish population, banks advertise a "Christmas or Hanukah Savings Club." In some communities there are Jewish organizations which try for "equal time" by having elaborate civic ceremonies for the Hanukah holiday. Families worried about the subliminal Christian aspect of the season—it is after all the birthday of Jesus—outdo Christmas with its one-day gift under the Christmas tree or in the stocking by making a fuss of gifts to the children on each of the eight days of the usually concurrent Hanukah holiday.

An Israeli four-year old, visiting in North America, sits in front of the television set. Unused to all-day TV, she gazes in rapt fascination. The time is between Thanksgiving and Christmas. Commercial after commercial tells her that life is incomplete if she does not buy X or do X for Christmas. At that point, she turns to her father, a puzzled look on her face. *"Abba, mah zeh Kreesmass?" Daddy, what is Christmas?*

That from an Israeli. The same question could have been asked about the Fourth of July or Thanksgiving; Diaspora Jews for the most part ask what is Yom Ha-Atzma'ut or Yom HaSho-ah.

The fact is that Diaspora Jews simply are not living a rhythm of life parallel to Israelis. The (American) Jewish cycle is muddy, unclear. E.L. Doctorow illustrates this in his novel about the era of the New York World's Fair (1939-1940). His insight of "then" is not so different from the reality of "now."

> Of course I knew virtually nothing about religion, beyond a few of the major Bible stories and the holidays associated with them. *I knew so far that most of the Jewish holidays were not as much fun as the regular ones. There was some forced insistence between them.* This was not true of the Fourth of July or New Year's or Thanksgiving. Purim, where you got apples and raisins and noisemakers and little blue-and-white flags, was sort of fun; and Chanukah, of course, where you got presents.*

Aside from confusing Simchat Torah and Purim, the writer makes the point well: "forced insistence." He continues with praise for Passover, "the giant of the Jewish holidays. . . . The story was good and the food was good."

Doctorow describes the two predominant and conflicting trends in the Jewish home of the day, a conflict which left its traces on the second generation. There is a leftist father, and a first-generation wife whose observance (lighting Sabbath candles) and activity in the Temple sisterhood coincide with her immigrant mother's death and her husband's straying. The immigrant generation and their children always had a sense of ambivalence about their Jewishness and their Americanism. In the case of Doctorow, the left-wing element "adjustment" is symbolized by the father.

The American Jewish left was an important factor, sometimes even a dominant factor, in Jewish life during many decades of this century,

---

* E.L. Doctorow, *World's Fair*, New York, Fawcett Crest: Ballantine Books, 1985, p. 129. (Italics added.)

especially in the '30s. It ranged from splinter Trotskyite bodies through "orthodox" Stalinists and on through Bundists (Yiddishist anti-Zionist socialists) and the various shades of Labor and Socialist-Zionists. The Yiddish newspaper, *Der Forverts* (Progress) had a tremendous impact on Jewish life until the decline of Yiddish in the 1950s and 60s.

Jews of a general labor coloration, not always specifically rooted in Jewish or Yiddish ideological movements were active in the trade unions as well. Many of them later entered Jewish community organizations as professionals, which, for a time, cast a certain way of thinking in these community and national groupings. The further left their origin, usually the more attenuated their Jewishness. Thus Jewish organizational life was dominated by a professional cadre of attenuated Jews, and an assimilated layer of Reform Jews who in the generations preceding World War II were still under the sway of classical Reform, ranging from outright anti-Zionism to indifference to Jewishness as a nationality.

Although Neo-Conservatism and Republicanism are vying for the support of Jews and, in some places, displacing the Democratic (or Liberal) party loyalty, the left-liberal Jewish world remains an ongoing force in the U.S. Jews on the whole still tend to see themselves as liberals and tend to support liberal candidates. Perhaps the most dramatic demonstration of this deeply ingrained characteristic which is sometimes subcutaneous, sometimes more apparent, is the leadership role of Jewish students in the 1968 anti-Vietnam movement.

Competing with this left-liberal universalist trend has been a strong sense of Jewish folk religion, an Americanized expression of the Eastern European traditional pattern. Herman Wouk is Orthodox, and his fictionalized memoir, *Inside Outside*, tells the story from a traditionalist view. What both have in common is the sense of differentness. Wouk's very title is the clue, as seen in this quote from the book: ". . . the Jewish thing from the start was inside the walls. Outside,. . . was the Goldene Medina, or Wicked America."*

Does the present generation feel this ambivalence? Is that ambivalence the key to Jewishness? Is that the basis of a new, quite dif-

---

* Herman Wouk, *Inside Outside*, New York, Avon Books, 1985, p. 48.

ferent sense of Galut, attenuated, yet somehow there? A middle-aged American Jew, visiting Israel for the first time, though her parents had been deeply involved in Israel's rebirth, said in the late 1980s: "Being in Israel I realize everyone here is Jewish. At home, I feel conscious of being a Jew, and am always aware of it." Her Israeli host then asked how her children feel about their Jewishness. She didn't know. "Probably not conscious," she thought. It would seem the subject had never been discussed.

Until the end of World War II, while the immigrant generation was still dominant, this "folk" force had great validity and strength. To a great extent, the war led to the full naturalization of the American Jew, as the native-born flocked to the colors. It also brought about a Jew who was more assertive in terms of his own Americanism and civil status. As against the anti-Semitism he may have met in the armed forces, there was the meritorious sense that he too had spilled blood or was ready to spill blood for his country.

World War II brought the Allied Jewish serviceman into face-to-face, horrifying contact with the concentration camps and aroused an almost atavistic identification with European Jews, as well as a fierce hatred of the Nazis. This led to a reaction of "gut Zionism" among many of the soldiers. Such factors strengthened the sense of a "national" ethnic identity among the Jews of North America. Over the past forty years, however, as American Jewry followed its own separate destiny, this has become weaker.

A seminar in Israel of senior professionals in a world-wide Jewish fundraising organization. As introductory lecturers, an Israeli and a North American speaker each present a view of the Diaspora. The Israeli is all gloom and doom: falling birthrate, diminishing communities, high intermarriage figures, immense assimilation. The North American speaks of flourishing new religious affiliation, stronger orthodoxy, vigorous Conservative and Reform movements, active community federations with increasing mobilization of younger leaders, improved Jewish education, increasing day-school enrollment, and so on.

The participants are, to put it mildly, confused. The situation is reminiscent of the old Yiddish conundrum, *Az s'iz azoi gut, farvoss iz azoy shlecht?* "If it's so good, why is it so bad?" And in true Talmudic fashion, comes a third party who is supposed to make sense of the first two. Summarizing, the third speaker says, "Both men spoke a truth. One speaks of the center, the other of the periphery. The center is gaining in strength, the periphery is falling away. We may end up with fewer Jews, but 'better' (i.e. more committed, even more knowledgeable!) Jews."

This is borne out by many studies, but perhaps most sharply indicated by a leading American Jewish professional, Dr. Steven Huberman, at the time director of research in a major Jewish federation in the U.S. "Roughly," he told the author, "fifty percent of the Jews here have no synagogue or organizational affiliation nor do they contribute to any Jewish organization or charity. Of the remaining fifty percent, about thirty-five percent do have some minimal connection, and about fifteen percent are actively involved in one or more facets of Jewish life." Later research show these figures as optimistic.

The question of course is how much of the periphery will fall away; how much center will remain? Is there a critical mass of numbers, or are Jews maintained simply by the idea of Jewishness and Judaism, as it seems they have been down the centuries? Can the saving remnant be a *saving* remnant without deep Jewish knowledge, without the Hebrew language, or the study of Torah, however Torah is interpreted or practiced? Is the cultural and social environment of American Jews even conducive to these considerations?

The fact that Jews are not affiliated or active, that there is a serious fall-off, is countered by those who see the future through different— rosier—spectacles. Among the latter is the author, Charles Silberman, whose thesis, baldly summarized, is that American Jews have "made it."* And since they have made it, socially, economically, educationally—in ways which can be measured externally—their future is assured. Jewish poverty measured in terms of Jewish knowledge is barely touched upon.

Silberman is not alone in being sanguine about the prospects of American Jewry. Other American sociologists and demographers agree that the Jewish population in America need not dwindle to infinitesimal

---

* Charles Silberman, *A Certain People: American Jews and their Lives Today*, New York, Summit Books, 1985.

numbers in two generations' time.* The Americans claim that intermarriage is not necessarily a net loss and that it may even lead to more active involvement by both the partner who converts and his or her spouse (the level of whose Jewish behavior may actually rise.)

Calvin Goldscheider writes about "new ethnic linkages" among Jews, which create the possibility of "ethnic cohesion." This cohesion ". . . finds its primary source in the structural conditions of job and social class, and not primarily in the search for ethnic identity or in the desire for group survival. . . ."**Calvin Goldscheider, *The American Jewish Community, Social Science Research and Policy Implications,* Atlanta, Scholars Press, 1986, published in cooperation with Israel-Diaspora Institute, Tel Aviv, p. 27. In layman's parlance, "Jews stick together," and in this case job and social class are an important part of the glue.

Without the glue of "the search for ethnic identity or . . . the desire for group survival," how long will the glue hold? And for how many? And what will be the quality of what remains?

---

* *The American Jewish Yearbook,* Vol. 89, Philadelphia, Jewish Publication Society, 1989, estimates the Jewish population in the United States at 5.935 million. Israeli demographers, however, foresee a significant decrease in the number of Jews in the United States by the year 2020. In *Basic Trends in American Jewish Demography,* New York, The American Jewish Committee, 1988, Profs. U.O. Schmelz & Sergio Dellapergola of the Hebrew University of Jerusalem project a Jewish population of 4.3 million Jews in the U.S. by the year 2020 based on "moderate net assimilatory losses"; or, a Jewish population of 3.7 million by 2020 based on "large net assimilatory losses."

** Calvin Goldschneider, *The American Jewish Community, Social Science Research and Policy Implications,* Atlanta, Scholars Press, 1986, published in cooperation with the Israel-Disapora Institute, Tel Aviv,p. 27.

CHAPTER SEVEN

THE ENVIRONMENT OF AMERICAN JEWS

All American Jews, whether assimilating, or involved and identified, live in a mass culture environment. To discuss "mass" erases differences. Mass does not relate to the intellectuals, the great university campuses, the outstanding pockets of art and culture in the general society. It ignores the centers of Jewish scholastic excellence, the seminaries and university departments of Jewish studies. It relates to the lowest common denominator.

Also ignored are the devoted thousands who search for greater Jewish meaning and content in their lives, who are aware that to be a Jew in the modern world is to swim against the stream of the mass culture and values which pervade the society in which they live. These include many of the leaders of synagogues and congregations, *havurot* (informal prayer or study groups) and of community federations, as well as the plethora of national and regional organizations. They are ignored not only because they are a small minority, but because their influence is circumscribed by the totality of the culture of which they are necessarily a part.

American family life seems to center around television.[1] In most homes, especially during periods of overlapping sports seasons, the weekend is—to a visitor—an endless binge of sport merging into sport. When championships are involved nothing else is the meat of discussion: in synagogue and meeting-places, on airplanes and at dinner tables. The poor American who couldn't care less about sports is just odd man out.

Television and movies are pushing America into what a *New York Times* opinion piece calls "postbabyism. . . . We no longer prefer the merely comic but now the explicitly moronic."* The games aspect of

---

* *The New York Times*, Opinion page, August 2, 1990.

American mass culture extends into business and politics. Profits are competitive; performance on the market is competitive. Some scholars believe that once entrepreneurs pass the threshold of comfort and financial security, money becomes merely a yardstick, a measuring rod, a way of keeping score. Career-planning is often called "your game-plan for life."

Politics is a bigger game, since it commands the largest screen. In presidential elections, the candidates' television confrontations were graded and ranked like thoroughbreds on a racing form-sheet. Television talk shows have created a standard of speech and affectation which applies from coast to coast. A visitor to the U.S. said in a lecture:

> If a visitor from Mars would watch television for any length of time, he would be sure that the world's major problems were personal hygiene; hair color; how to save pennies on groceries and dollars on cars; how to make money fast by answering inane questions; and again and again—personal hygiene: smells, sheen, shape. If he watched the spy and detective shows, or the comedies ("sitcoms"), he would be convinced that every problem in the world can be solved within the slot of half-an-hour.

As the *New York Times* op-ed piece put it:

> Postbabyism is particularly rampant in television advertising where merely by changing a cassette tape or tossing a coin in a fountain, the characters can fulfill their postbaby dreams—no boss, no work, postbaby bottles filled with beer and babes, adult babes, to play with.

Television news during the Gulf War was presented like a sales

---

* Percy Walker in *Love in the Blue Ruins* (New York, Dell, 1971), p. 220 puts the following social comment in the mouth of a not-so-mad "madman":
  Did you know that there are three thousand and fifty-one TV and radio announcers in the South, of which (sic!) twenty-two hundred are from Ohio, and that every last one of these twenty-two hundred says "the difference between he and I." In twenty years we'll all be talking like that.

competition designed to win viewers from other channels by peddling war fever, maudlin pity for the hostages. The channels rode the "our-boys-out-there" train to its last station, and mindlessly provided screen time for Saddam Hussein—*all in the most cynical and misleading way.* There were some serious reports and discussion, but well-concealed under the bombast of "**War in the Middle East?? . . . . Kuwait update!**" delivered in tones which would shame Orson Welles.

A *Los Angeles Times* report based on a study by the Council for Foreign Relations derided American television networks' foreign coverage as *"sporadic, superficial, [lacking in] perspective. . . crisis-driven and [the reflector] of a misleading picture of the world and America's place in it."**

De Gaulle is supposed to have said, after visiting Rio, "Le Brésil, ce n'est pas serieux": Brazil just isn't a serious place. Visitors might make the same mistake about the U.S. But visitor, take care! The American style covers a content of immense power and ability as well as intellectual wealth spread much wider than one sees at first sight. But, while Jews are certainly part of the intellectual power and ability of America, organized Jewish life does not function anywhere near the highest common denominator.

Why? There is probably more than one reason. Jews as Jews do not have total responsibility for the politics, economy, society or culture. They make their contribution or have an impact as individuals. Sometimes they are viewed as Jews, often—usually—just as Americans. As a group, the polity is not theirs, therefore the seriousness and full weight of the polity is not theirs alone. Individual Jews may take disproportionate responsibility in public life and may be outstanding or highly visible in certain fields. But they generally see their role as Americans, without any hyphens. Good performance then may bring honor to their Jewishness, however defined, but that is the extent of it. These American Jews in politics, government or on campus are often not active in the Jewish community, which offers them a smaller stage. If they do participate in the organized life of the community, they must play according to the rules of the game, which strives for a median level, as in all establishments, which prefer the mediocre. The ancient Athenians

---

* Carried in *The Jerusalem Post*, December 16, 1990, p. 5. Emphasis added.

ostracized the unique; organizations generally, and politics today tend to shun the innovators.

Jewish organizational life centers on the rich who can finance the organizations which have elicited their allegiance. Though U.S. Jews are better educated than ever, their social style and taste reflect that of their general class and caste. The aristocracy of learning has yielded pride of place to the plutocracy of wealth. The rabbis and professional leaders are usually if not always part of the system—must be in order to survive—and often share its values. If they do not, their role is circumscribed indeed.

"MAKING IT"

Some American writers have already been quoted with variations on the theme that "the Jews have never had it so good" as they have in the United States. Certainly to judge by objective factors, the percentage of Jews attaining college education, for example, is higher than the percentage of the general population: 90%, possibly even 95%. Never has such a large percentage of Jews had the option of such unlimited educational opportunity.

Similarly, the economic level of American Jews is remarkable in comparison to the general population.

> . . . Jews are disproportionately concentrated in professional and managerial occupations and among those who have postgraduate levels of education. These socioeconomic levels characterize the Jewish population in America in ways which differentiate Jews from non-Jews. Indeed, *the occupational and educational disparities between Jews and non-Jews have increased over time.* *

In the political sphere, Jews have reached high visibility and major roles. There has been a Jewish Secretary of State, and in 1989 there were eight Jewish Senators (out of 100 members of the Senate) and 31

---

* Calvin Goldschneider, *The American Community, Social Science Research and Policy Implications* (Atlanta, Scholars Press, 1986), p. 24, also in *Jewish Continuity and Change* (Bloomington, Indiana University Press, 1986), pp. 115-6. Emphasis added.

Jewish Representatives out of a total of 431 members of the House. As in the storybooks, somewhere a Jewish man or woman is planning to become America's first Jewish President, and after all, dreams are the stuff from which reality is woven.

The situation in Canada is not so different. Given the innate conservatism of the Canadians and more visible anti-Semitism, the dream of a Jewish Prime Minister is further away than that of the Presidency south of the border. There have been Jews in highly visible positions, such as Governor of the Bank of Canada, senior cabinet ministers, senators, as well as Jewish premiers of provinces.

All of which goes to say that the Americanism of U.S. Jews (Canadianism of Canadian Jews) is enhanced by a wide-open society. Jews can dream what was—in other countries throughout history and in more distant American history—"the Impossible Dream."

ATTITUDES OF AMERICAN JEWS TOWARD THEMSELVES

If American Jews have made it, what do such American Jews believe about themselves and their situation? This writer's view is one from the outside—if not the man from Mars—at least the man from Israel. How does an insider see these issues? Professor Gerald Bubis is an experienced participant and observer, and shared the following thoughts with a Jerusalem audience.*

> The shores of America, especially in the peak period of 1880-1920 represented to American Jewish immigrants the new Zion, the new Jerusalem, similar to the experience of the Pilgrims. For the first time, one could be as little Jewish as one wished without having to pay the price of admission by becoming someone or something else. Jews could simply be Americans and Jews. These conditions created a new historical phenomenon.
>
> America is the only place where structural, official, or legis-

---

* The notes of Professor Bubis's lectures in the summer of 1988 were taken by Ms. Ruth Borison, with his permission to cite him in this book. Bubis was for many years Director of the School for Jewish Social Service at Hebrew Union College, Los Angeles.

lative anti-Semitism has never existed. Anti-Semitism has never posed a serious threat. Western European countries basically are composed of a mono-cultural, mono-religious society with one ethnic background, one language and one value system. The emphasis placed on ethnicity and geography is totally unlike anything in the American experience. Therefore there exists no basis for comparison between the two experiences.

Never in history (not even during Spain's Golden Age) did Jews achieve such high offices. If anything, Jews in the U.S. are being "loved to death." Some Jewish leaders perversely wish there existed more anti-Semitism as a vehicle toward uniting the Jews, activating them, and rallying them around a common cause or fear.

ANTI-SEMITISM

Even if it "does not pose a serious threat," most American Jews realize anti-Semitism exists. A number of large "defense" organizations take combatting anti-Semitism as a major or sole plank in their platform, and massive sums are expended to monitor the media and to research anti-Semitic incidents, and then to respond or organize responses.* Part of the neurosis of American Jews, and perhaps of Jews in general, is the ambivalence between the need to recognize, face and combat anti-Semitism, and the desire to play it down: "It's not that bad. . . or as dangerous as it used to be."

In a way, the battle enhances the American identity of the Jew: ". . . civil Judaism's emphasis on countering anti-Semitism. . . and on supporting Israel. . . enables the American Jew to feel (s)he is contributing to Jewish survival without materially affecting his/her lifestyle or position in American society.**

The linking of anti-Semitism and support for Israel is not accidental.

---

* These include the American Jewish Committee, the Anti-Defamation League (ADL) of B'nai B'rith, the Community Relations Councils and its national organization, and the American Jewish Congress. "Defense" in this sense is used as countering public manifestations of anti-Semitism through legal means and the media, and does not involve or imply physical action.

** Woocher, p. 99.

The existence of Israel is seen by many Jews as a bulwark against anti-Semitism. Some of the older generation and some of the younger Jews—children of Holocaust survivors, or who see themselves in the light of Elie Wiesel's statement "We are all survivors"—refer to Israel as an "insurance policy."

Fear of anti-Semitism was a major factor not only in maintaining Jewish identity over the decades; in the earlier part of this century it was the motive force for the creation of the "classical" Jewish defense organizations mentioned earlier. In the Zionist-tinted ideology and rhetoric of Jewish leaders, the following thesis was propounded: We are hated, feared, or "under suspicion" because we are "different" or "abnormal."

Normalcy in the sense of acceptable American ethnicity means having an "original homeland" to which the ethnic group can relate: Ireland, Germany, Sweden, etc. A parallel situation has developed among black Americans with regard to Africa. The euphemism "man of color" became successively: colored, Negro, black, Afro-American and most recently in a speech in Zambia, Jesse Jackson proposed calling American blacks "African-Americans."* Creating a Jewish homeland in "Palestine"—as Zionists referred to it then—would make the Jews in America equivalent to other ethnic groups which had a geographic base, a national address, a land to which they could relate.

American Jews today are still preoccupied with anti-Semitism. In a study by Professor Steven M. Cohen, an overwhelming majority of the respondents—better than four-to-one—agreed that "anti-Semitism in America may, in the future, become a serious problem". More than half did not agree with the statement that anti-Semitism was "currently not a serious problem." Interestingly, younger adults in the study were much less likely to perceive American anti-Semitism than their elders.** Jewish political clout, readiness to tackle the media, as well as the effectiveness of highly organized and well-oiled "defense" organizations tend to make the Jew feel safer, at home, almost at ease.

---

* Cited by Flora Lewis in the *International Herald Tribune*, January 12, 1989, Opinion page, "Jesse Jackson: A Cannon That Often Shoots True."
** Steven M. Cohen, *Ties and Tensions: The 1986 Survey of American Jewish Attitudes Toward Israel and Israelis*, New York, The American Jewish Committee, 1987.

Yet. . . some Jews still lower their voices in public places when saying "Jew" or discussing Jewish affairs; others squirm when obviously Jewish names appear in criminal or treason trials. Jewish insecurity, sometimes helped by covert or overt anti-Semitism, tends to make Jews more aware of their Jewishness when a fellow Jew breaks civil and social taboos or public mores. The examples range from the Rosenberg atomic espionage case to the pate of insider-trading prosecutions.

On a visit to the U.S. in August 1989, the author was surprised to hear two leading personalities in a major Jewish community say that they felt there might be an anti-Semitic conspiracy fostered by circles in the American government. As proof, they cited the severity of punishment meted out to the Pollards, as well as the scope and anti-Jewish innuendoes surrounding the securities trading cases. Both men are experienced communal figures, and not prone to hysteria. In England, with the Guiness case, anti-Jewish statements in the press were even more explicit.

There exists, then, in the American Jewish psyche an amalgam of discomfort, suspicion and sensitivity, together with a measure of low self-esteem and occasional self-hatred. But, there is another side to that picture: it's "in" to be or act Jewish. Especially is this true in certain professions such as music, the arts and academia, particularly in the larger urban centers. Thus in New York and Los Angeles, where the arts and media have such influence and from which they emanate to all of North America and beyond, to assume supposedly Jewish behavior traits, and to use Yiddishisms and Yiddish intonations are part of the scene. Again, a look at fiction:

> "I've often wished I were Jewish," [the heroine is speaking]. . . . "In fact, I do wish that." Wonderful exotic Jewish parents, instead of so-ordinary Florence and Harry, she is thinking disloyally.
> "It would be interesting to know how many people share our wish," says [the hero]. . . .*

---

* In Alice Adams, *Superior Women*, New York, Ballantine Books, 1985, p. 173.

In all of these areas, competition also brings out the ugly side of the coin: Truman Capote's talk of the Jewish literary mafia; a university professor's remarks to a mainly WASP class about foreign policy consultants and professors who say, "Ve Amerricans," a snide reference to Henry Kissinger. Can all the success make up for the existential marginality which so many Jews feel? Of late, anti-Semitism is on the increase, as measured in incidents and in the media. Patrick Buchanan's columns and TV appearances have not been very friendly towards people with Jewish names or to Israel. * WiththeUnitedStatesbeingin what may be a lengthy period of economic recession or very slow recovery, and the grim mood of drift and resentment towards the political establishment which characterizes U.S. life, anti-Semitism is mounting. White supremacists of varied ilks are riding a new crest of interest, while black anti-Semitism is a powerful factor yet to be fully revealed. The 1990s may prove to create a different attitude towards anti-Semitism, and writers in this decade may have to be far less sanguine than in the 80s.

Anti-Semitism has always been a powerful factor in "enhancing" Jewish identity. Similarly, ethnicism engenders ethnicism. The American Third World, especially its dispossessed blacks, is the spawning grounds for a new and virulent anti-Semitism, and Farrakhan's explicit Jew hatred may reveal much of what others in that deprived under class feel. The rapid increase in the Muslim population in the U.S. through conversion, immigration and a high birthrate probably presages further increase of anti-Semitism.

Ultimately, against the backdrop of the historic Jewish memory, the question, often unspoken, lies below the surface. How safe is safe? Polls cannot reveal the answer, when so many forgotten memories, historic associations and twistings of the soul exist. . . .

SUPPORT FOR ISRAEL IS AMERICAN

Justice Louis D. Brandeis, much admired by his Jewish compatriots on his elevation to the Supreme Court in 1916, the first Jew to hold that office, said, "To be good Americans, we must be better Jews, and to be

---

* This was written well before Buchanan became a failed presidential candidate.

better Jews we must be Zionists."* Brandeis was telling American Jews that their Jewishness was compatible with "Americanism," and that to be Jewish was to be a Zionist.

American Zionism was essentially a movement for other Jews, basically for European Jews whose fate and future were in danger. (The old definition was: A Zionist is a Jew who collects money from a second Jew so a third Jew can go to Palestine.) Only the *halutz* ("pioneer") youth organizations of the Zionist movement, mainly founded by emigrants from Eastern Europe preached and to some extent practiced *aliyah,* "making the ascent" to live in Palestine as immigrants.**

In the years following statehood, philanthropic Zionism evolved a pathos and an ideology of sorts as the United Jewish Appeal undertook the task of raising funds for Israeli and other purposes. The appeal was made together with local Jewish federations for domestic purposes as well as for what is called by the cognoscenti, "overseas." Codes were developed which really stand for a balancing of interests on at least two levels.

On one level, various interest groups in the community such as the Jewish community center, the old age home, family service and—increasingly over the last years—Jewish schools, all make their claim for the philanthropic dollar. This is countered by an Israel lobby or a Joint (Joint Distribution Committee) lobby, which sometimes work in tandem. The Joint focuses on "Jews in distress"—Jews in countries like Iran or Eastern Europe. The Israel lobby pushes for increased budgeting for the Jewish Agency for Israel.

On another level, since these are voluntary organizations devoted to and based on raising funds, they must present their message so that it will match the presumed interest of their contributors. What will interest

---

* *The Curse of Bigness*, Miscellaneous papers of Louis D. Brandeis, New York, Viking Press, 1934.
** In modern Hebrew, *Halutz* means pioneer, but in the Bible (*Deut.* 3:18) it probably meant lightly-armed infantry, stripped down of heavy armament for freedom of maneuver. They were the shock troops of the day, "those who go before the camp." The modern usage is not related to the military; most Zionist youth movements were influenced by social idealism and took the kibbutz as their model.

and "sell" its clientele becomes the "appeal" of the Appeal. For many years, the main thrust of Appeal publicity has been Israel: immigration and its concomitant problems, land development and settlement, neighborhood renewal, youth education.

Political and military issues which cannot be addressed by the campaigns since the funds gathered are limited by tax regulation to charitable use, have nonetheless often provided the stimuli for interest and concern. These stimuli are then exploited by the fundraisers, both voluntary and professional, to increase the amounts pledged.

A cursory review of income from the United Jewish Appeal to Israel shows that there were quantum leaps with the dramatic (and tragic) moments of war: The Six-Day War in 1967 and the Yom Kippur War in 1973, obviously less in the 1982 Galilee War, and then again more for "Operation Moses" and "Operation Solomon" (the Ethiopian immigration) and "Operation Exodus" which is the name for the Russian immigration.*

What does this mean? It means that the fundraisers relate to the more acute problem *of the day*; the readiness of more Jews to give more money has been in direct proportion to the visibility of danger to Israel or to Jews elsewhere (Ethiopia, the former USSR for example). It further means that many contributors have been trained to give more on a community-centered orientation as the overseas and Israel problems become less acute or newsworthy.

Raising money for "overseas"— as Israel and Jews in danger are called in the community code — when the situation is sufficiently dramatic shows both a high and low level of commitment. Why the paradox? If people perceive danger and react to it with generosity, how can this be a "low level of commitment?" The criticism is not pointed at the intense reaction in times of danger, but rather at the withering away of involvement in times of relative normalcy. Crisis-pro-Israelism or crisis-Zionism indicates that many of the large contributors and numbers

---

* The funds of the UJA for use in Israel are actually paid over to the United Israel Appeal, which makes the transfers and monitors their use in accordance with U.S. Internal Revenue Service Regulations. However, such details of its work are known more to the officers of local federations and other involved people, rather than to the general public.

of small givers do not see the campaign as an instrument of "people-building" or a "voluntary tax." In order to arouse passion, some Jewish leaders and some campaign publicity often become emotionally strident in times of politico-military tensions, over-adulatory in time of triumph (such as the successful transfer of Ethiopian Jews to Israel), or paternalistic about the economic and social status of Israel's citizens.

The latter is especially evident in the sentimental and facile slogans around poverty, backwardness, lack of amenities—all aimed at arousing guilt and ultimately resulting in condescension. By working at the lowest common denominator of "charity," of "helping those who cannot help themselves," of "we have everything while our fellow Jews have so little," and the like, false emotions are fostered and stroked. The truth is poorly served. The educational and ideological messages are sorely missed. Often, Israeli representatives help foster these reactions.

So, among the many ambivalences in the Israel/Diaspora relationship, there is love of Israel, pity for Israel; respect for the heroic Israel, condescension for the poor and backward Israel.

Levi Eshkol, that wise and earthy mentsch, was blessed by a sense of humor unusual in politicians. As a former Finance Minister, and as Israel's Prime Minister after the stunning victory of the Six-Day War, he was aware of the dichotomy between Israel's power and the "need" to encourage fundraising by projecting Israel's weaknesses. He coined the phrase, "Shimshon der Nebechdiker"—Samson the weakling, the nebbish.

Perhaps there is less ambivalence for pro-Israeli and Zionist Jews when Israel is viewed as needy, backward and dependent. There is, then, simple justification for not wanting to live there for that very small group who seek justification, a noble rationale for remaining in the Diaspora: to help keep Israel strong. Pity and love are often closely related feelings, but pity implies arm's length, and may mask a sense of superiority. And yet, the Yoni Netanyahu-Entebbe saga and the Ari Ben Canaan syndrome (made famous in Leon Uris's *Exodus*) also involves hero worship. (Netanyahu was the commander of the Israeli force which rescued Jewish hostages from the Arab terrorist highjacking of an Air France plane at Entebbe, Uganda on July 4, 1976. He was wounded in action and died in the plane returning the force and their liberated hostages to Israel. Ari Ben Canaan was created by Uris in the image of the New Jew [Israeli] warrior and man of action, strong, silent and brave.) Hero worship of the Israeli, and gratitude for wiping out the historic calumny that Jews are cowards. . . and a sigh of relief: "Thank God my son doesn't have to do that."

The decades-old story recounted in Zionist youth groups is the reaction of the irate parent, confronted by his/her offspring who has decided to live in Israel: "Fifty years a Zionist, and it had to happen to me. . . ." Or, this classic and quite true statement made by an American Jewish mother at the "graduation parade" of her son the paratrooper in Israel. As the son dropped down out of the sky, the mother moaned: "That's a job for a Jewish boy?"

Ambivalence towards Israel has been compounded by a number of recent crises: the Lebanese War (Peace for Galilee), the *intifada*, Israel government settlement policy, and the "Who is a Jew?" issue. Part of this ambivalence has been caught very well in an otherwise extremely poor novel:

> . . . I can look at you and tell your political position straight off [an ex-American living in Israel tells his visiting college friend]. Basic internationalist. Sympathy with Zionism but substantially against it. To you the whole thing is a tragedy. . . Hitler killed the Jews, forced them to flee. They came here and now, out of their desperate need to survive, they've turned into mini-despots of their own, perhaps not Nazis but nothing to be proud of. . . .
>
> . . . You don't like the militarism of the state, the economic reliance on arms sales, the aid to South Africa and the contras, the treatment of Palestinian refugees, Ashkenazi prejudice against Sephardim and vice versa, the spying on the U.S., the pervasive fundamentalism, the conservative social structure and the decline of the socialist ideal.*

Political disagreement with Israel's policies by liberals has fanned growing disaffection from Israel, even among Jews who are involved in the community and have a very positive attitude towards Israel. One phrased it this way: "There is a large group of American Jews who do not believe that Israel is germane to their security and safety." With the

---

* Roger L. Simon, *Raising the Dead*, New York, Villard Books, 1988, p. 124.

ascension of Labor to power, it is the turn of the right and the neo-con-
servatives to criticize Israeli government policies as over-eager to make
concessions to the Arabs.

---

1. Israel may be accused of similar ways. Beyond the ideological differences
and societal aims, there are technical factors which until 1993 reduced
somewhat the influence of mass culture: fewer television hours, little choice
of channels, a different tradition in the press and TV (also changing under
the relentless example of America), and the fact that thirty percent of Israelis
range from very observant orthodox Jews to ultra-orthodox, who are not
"permitted" by their spiritual leaders to watch television or own TV sets.

However, in 1993, the introduction of cable TV and a commercial second
channel increases the danger to Israeli culture. Nonetheless, there are always
surprises. In *Yediot Aharonot*, February 12, 1993, a report showed that 55%
of the readers of Israel's most important four dailies usually never read the
sports page. Forty-five percent don't read the literary pages. All major
Hebrew dailies publish outstanding literary supplements on Fridays, and
HaAretz a literary supplement on Wednesdays as well.

CHAPTER EIGHT

AMERICAN JEWRY:
COMPLETING THE PICTURE

A growing number of the community leadership in the U.S. hold that American Jewry is now coming of age. This maturity is borne out, they believe, by the fact that the community is no longer totally outer-directed: taking most of its cues from Israel's problems. The agenda it pursues is increasingly independent, grounded in indigenous American perceptions.

This may be seen in the differences of opinion on decisions taken by Israel as opposed to those of the American Jewish community. Some examples are the dropout phenomenon among Soviet Jews;* how to handle the Pollard affair fallout; and of course the question of "Who is a Jew." Most telling perhaps is—with the exception of "Operation Exodus" to finance the migration of ex-Soviet Jews to Israel—the falling proportion of allocations to "Israel" (to the Jewish Agency) out of total funds raised by the local Jewish federations.

The question is whether this is a true coming of age in the American Jewish community, or a function of Israel's increasing maturity. Is it—more likely—a concentration on more immediate problems, those of financing the institution or service "around the corner" or next door, as opposed to one six or nine thousand miles away? Most observers believe that the American Jewish community has become increasingly self-centered, and hence parochial in its interests. This has been paralleled by a declining interest in Israel. Time has had its effect. We live today over two generations after the

---

* The drop-outs were Soviet Jews who, in the late 1980s, left the Soviet Union on Israeli visas, supposedly bound for Israel, but who "dropped out" in Vienna and Rome (Ladispoli) to wait in their thousands until they could obtain entry visas to the United States.

Holocaust, two generations after the rise of the State. We are over one generation from the Six-Day War, and close to another whole generation of growing nationalism in Israel following the rise to power of the Likud, and the concomitant increased power of the ultra-orthodox.

A community that has achieved maturity and autonomy takes the necessary symbols for its life out of the reality it has itself experienced. An American Jewish academic, Professor Jacob Neusner, has written:

> Perhaps it appears ironic that a book on American Judaism begins with the encounter with the State of Israel. But the irony is only for a Jew who is no Zionist. . . . the two events [the Holocaust and the establishment of Israel] constitute the generative myth by which the generality of American Jews make sense of themselves and decide what to do with that part of themselves set aside for 'being Jewish.' "*

This was written over two decades ago. Yet generative myths do not usually fade. The question is whether parents have succeeded in conveying these myths to children, or what the present young generation have inherited to help them "make sense of themselves" and how much is "that part of themselves set aside for 'being Jewish.' "

From a certain Zionist perspective, the durability of the Diaspora, more, its undoubted accomplishments, are an embarrassment. Classic Zionism tragically had an easy analysis. Beginning with the European Jewish condition, and finding it mostly wanting, Zionist ideology set forth the prognosis that in Exile things could only get worse.

This was not a Zionist invention. For the notion that God had punished His people, exiling them to the ends of the earth, was a tenet borrowed from traditional Judaism. The Zionist innovation was that the chronic malady which had lasted twenty centuries had now entered its

---

* Jacob Neusner, *Stranger At Home: The Holocaust, Zionism, and American Judaism.* Chicago: University of Chicago Press, 1981.

terminal stage. If the Jews didn't "get" a homeland, Exile would "get" them. The Immortal People would become mortal like all others. The choice was between two deaths, by pogrom's sword in the East, or by assimilation's kiss in the West.

America is founded on just the opposite premise. Israel is a national solution for a people, it is a mono-cultural solution. The Israeli passport identifies its citizens immediately (if not always correctly) as Jewish. This was Zionism's purpose. Chaim Weizmann, then President of the World Zionist Organization, and later Israel's first President, said to the Versailles Peace Conference *after World War I*, "Our aim is to make Palestine as Jewish as Britain is British, France French, and Italy Italian." Each example is of a *national state*.

America is a multi-cultural, multi-racial society of citizenship. Its solution for "poor and huddled masses" is a new non-national or cross-ethnic society. To see a U.S. passport is to know nothing of its bearer in terms of ethnic derivation, religion or cultural milieu. America is a state of citizenship, Ben Gurion would say, rather than of nationality. A Rothschild, he mused, could be a Frenchman for 200 years and in the eyes of the French be seen in a sense as a stranger, a Jew. To be French is to be part of a people and a majority language and culture based on Catholicism. Not so America. Though Christian in a general sense, it is certainly more and more multi-ethnic and—to the dismay of some Americans— multi-cultural and multi-linguistic.

Before World War II, few Zionists imagined the ruthless extent to which the first half of their prognosis would be realized in the Final Solution. That left the Jews of the West. To the discomfiture of ideologues, Jewry seemed to be alive if not completely well in Terre Haute, Cardiff, Medicine Hat and other *shtetlach*; all settled mainly by Eastern European pre-Holocaust survivors.

THE NUMBERS GAME

Then demographers came to the rescue of flagging Zionist doctrine. Death by the kiss of assimilation would yet vindicate the grim prediction. In the early 1980s, the *American Jewish Yearbook* revealed that the percentage of Jews in the American population had dropped by one-third (from a high of 3.7% at the zenith in 1937 to 2.54%).* The projection sees a continued and steep decline. If these numbers come close to reality then the American Jewish population is smaller by 2.5 million than it would have been had the 1937 proportion held. Gone, too, is the small-comfort mythical number of six million American Jews, a mirror of the unbearable catastrophe of European Jewry almost half-a-century earlier.

One may well ask: Will there be enough Jews to maintain a rich communal and thriving Jewish life? Or will American Jews settle for sheer survival, for the minimal ability to maintain Jewish institutions? This is particularly true about an educational network which does not produce the Hebrew teachers or "religious school" teachers required for either the day-school system or the supplementary (afternoon and Sunday) schools. It may also be true of rabbis and communal workers. Will shrinking numbers and demographic changes decrease the political clout needed to influence American policy both to defend Israeli interests and those of American Jews themselves?

Although doom-sayers said it earlier, hard evidence to support the notion of a depleted American Jewish population was spotty until 1970.** Then the bad news made its way on the back of intermarriage figures. It was reported that 41% of Jewish males married spouses not born Jews. The early 1990s saw the figures pass 50% and even 60%. However, some do not see only doom.

For example, it was taken for granted that inevitably rising education, occupation, income, and the attendant status could only result in greater assimilation. This may not be so inevitable. Despite the incredible *embarras de richesse* of American Jews, they remain different in family structure, political behavior and social attitudes from other Americans.

What is there to assimilate to? For better or for worse, the very

---

* Sidney Goldstein, "Jews in the United States: Perspectives and Demography," *AJYB*, vol. 81, 1981. Followed two years later by U.O. Schmelz and Sergio Dellapergola, "The Demographic Consequences of U.S. Population Trends," *AJYB*, vol. 83, 1983.
** National Jewish Population Survey, 1970–1971.

breakup of the cultural hegemony of the WASPs and the growth of ethnicity as a legitimate dimension have forced the politicization of group identity.*

The question is, though, whether politicization of Jewishness carries with it enough substance and content for the future generations. Can Jewishness without a religious commitment and knowledge of Judaism, or a deep connection with Israel carry Jewish identity forward another few generations?

SUPPORT FOR ISRAEL

Not only does support for Israel appear to be a chief function of Jewish communal organizations, but

> .... this support almost fully defines the range of interests of Jewish community organizations in politics. At the same time, Israel occupies a major place in the content of Jewish life; it defines much of the curriculum of Jewish schools, and much of the subject matter of the Jewish sermon.**

In other words remove or reduce support for Israel and you put Jewish affiliation and even Jewish identity in jeopardy. Is this a vindication of Zionism's assumption that life in the Diaspora was doomed? Or are the implications that there is no inherent Jewish content to American Jewry, nor is there a significance other than obstinacy to continued survival? Again, the question seems to bring us back to the issue of Jewish knowledge and content for commitment.

Woocher believes that

> Israel has become a symbol in which the entire world-view

---

* Daniel Bell, "Where Are We?" Moment Magazine, May 1986.
** Nathan Glazer, "New Perspectives in American Jewish Sociology," New York, American Jewish Committee, 1987. An anecdote may better illustrate this. A popular Miami rabbi was noted for his overwhelming Zionism, and every Friday night—with few exceptions—spoke about Israel. One evening, a parishioner asked, "Rabbi, what's the sermon about this week? Something else?"

and ethos of American Jewish civil religion are crystallized. . . . Further, to help Israel survive. . . is nothing less than a "sacred covenant". . . . Thereby they act to ensure their own historic significance as well.*

There is, however no reciprocity.

American love for Israel can be turned from a gift to be treasured into a curiosity to be exploited. . . . "Don't worry about the American Jews, who are neither real Americans or real Jews, who are most of all not serious people; their sentimental attachment to Israel is so essential to them, to their own sense of identity, that they will finally accept whatever we say or do."**

As the leadership of the American Jewish community perceives this cavalier Israeli attitude, resentment grows, and it bodes ill.

Summing up his contemporary review of the interplay between assimilation and numbers, Nathan Glazer writes:

However the matter is put, what we are in fact asking is whether American Jewry is headed for assimilation or whether it is engaged in transforming the terms in which Jewishness and Judaism are to be understood. . . . Is there a straight-line process of reduction in Jewish knowledge, commitment to Jewish causes, involvement in the Jewish religion, connection to the Jewish community—American or international—with each passing generation. . . . or is there, rather. . . . the emergence of something new?

We add a question to that of Glazer's and ask, if something new is emerging, will it be recognized as Jewish outside of America? This question obviously does not concern North America alone. It applies equally to all open societies.

---

* Woocher, cited pp. 78–80.
** Leonard Fein, "Who is a Jew? Covenant and Contract," *Forum on the Jewish People, Zionism and Israel*, 62, Winter/Spring, Jerusalem 1989.

In brief, the Diaspora Jewish community is suffering from acute hemorrhaging in terms of numbers. For those remaining as identified Jews, will anti-Semitism, ethnicism, and a new form of Jewishness ("something new") give the bulk of the community enough forward motion to exist as a recognizable Jewish community a few generations down the road? Below we have some indication of today's problems in identity which may shed some light on the future. . . .

JEWISH IDENTITY AMONG THE NON-ORTHODOX AND NON-AFFILIATED

What maintains Jewish identity among non-orthodox Jews in the Diaspora? Among the non-affiliated, a phenomenon of shrinking allegiance can be observed, yet there are vestigial traces of Jewish identity. In the cases cited below, the reasons for this tenuous association are a combination of forces, both recognizable and subliminal. Some are not American examples, but certainly parallel the American experience. They also demonstrate that the situation is world-wide.

Claude is a first-generation French Jew married to a non-Jewish woman.* His last name—Birnbaum—makes it difficult to hide or ignore his roots. Helping to bolster this inner identity are his parents' tales of persecution in Poland and their life in collaborationist Vichy France where they took refuge during World War II. He is himself familiar with French anti-Semitism. There is pride in Israel's prowess in the "good" days, resentment at the French media's treatment of Israel. He and his wife have visited Israel a number of times.

The couple's friends are Jewish: neither the Birnbaums nor their wives keep any minimal Jewish observance in their home or lifestyle. Their children's friends are not Jewish which increases the likelihood that they will marry out of the faith. The third generation from the ghetto may see the end of the Birnbaums. They may retain the family name. They could become "Poirier." If they do keep Birnbaum, they may be like the Cohens of Birmingham.

Philip Cohen is a third-generation British Jew. His grandmother

---

* The names in the text have been changed.

was not Jewish, nor was his mother. In light of those two generations, and according to the majority opinion in Jewish practice today, neither he nor his father would be considered Jewish. For some reason, the family retained a link to the Jewish community. Perhaps it was the name. Birnbaum might sound Alsatian or German to a Frenchman, but Cohen is *the* primordial Hebrew name, going back to Aharon the Cohen (the priest,) the brother of Moses.* Perhaps it was the fact that the business in which the family worked involved many Jews.

Through these tenuous links, eventually Philip was discovered by a recruiter for an Israel-centered fundraising organization. He became active in the campaign; he and his wife have visited Israel often, have a child married to an Israeli, and Philip is active—actually a leader—in sponsoring Jewish education in his home city.

These stories could be multiplied by hundreds, by thousands, but little research has been done on the unidentified or unaffiliated Jews of the West, and less on those of the former Soviet Union. In both cases, (and many more this writer is familiar with), Israel plays a role in fanning the historic tie.

Emanuel Azenberg, the Broadway producer who grew up in the home of an active and committed Labor Zionist father, admits this was a background

> which I marginally paid attention to. I was an American kid playing in the streets of the Bronx and his commitment wasn't my commitment. But I went to a Labor Zionist camp in the summer, and the idea of this country [Israel] became part of my identity. . . .
>
> My wife is not Jewish, so halachically neither are my

---

* See *Exodus* 21:1 ff. In Italy some Cohens have Italianized their name over the long generations of Jewish presence in that country, and are Sacerdote. (The latter delights those who recall high-school or college Latin.) Perhaps the name Levi outranks Cohen as a "trade" or family name, since this was Moses and Aharon's tribe. The word Jew comes from Judah, one of the twelve sons of Jacob. But Jacob's name became Israel, when he returned to Palestine (*Genesis* 32:29).

children; but Rivka Ilana Azenberg and Yehudit Hanna Azenberg are not going to walk about Irish.*

The point is that the statistical truth of today may not be the historic truth of tomorrow. Notwithstanding the potential of cases such as these, the tenuous links of the less identified and the unaffiliated present a true, imminent and *growing* danger to Jewish numbers in the future.

CONVERTS, MARGINAL JEWS AND RESIDUAL JEWS

The debate goes on. Is intermarriage between Jews and non-Jews bleeding the Jewish people of its numbers? Is it adding to its numbers? The subject is dissected by journalists and sociologists. But it is lived, debated, discussed, hushed up or hidden, depending on the *dramatis personae*, by rabbis, teachers, and most important within families. From *Tevyeh der Milchiger* (that Tuvia the Milkman who became transformed from Shalom Aleichem's Yiddish-speaking, Bible-misquoting character to a world-wide media star through *Fiddler on the Roof*), to last night's holiday or Friday night family dinner, the non-Jewish mate is vivisected, the new situation analyzed.

Guilt ("I gave him/her the best possible Jewish education. . . He/she is not Jewish but so nice. . . He/she isn't that special, why couldn't he/she have found a good Jewish boy/girl"), and compensating pride ("He/she's a better Jew than our son/daughter. . . Their child goes to a Jewish day school. . . You should hear the little one say the *motzi* [opening grace or blessing over bread]"—there is no end of mixed emotions.

Mixed marriages = mixed emotions: the new Jewish law of relativity.

Beyond the converts are the marginal Jews, who retain an element of Jewish identity or connection. This may range from "feeling Jewish" or some recalled observance of Jewish customs or relationship to Jewish institutions, to a residual and all but unexpressed identity.

---

* *The Jerusalem Post*, Television Plus Entertainment Section, June 19, 1992, 3B.

He is a second-generation North American. Married for the second time to a non-Jewish Baltic type, whom his grandparents and parents would unquestioningly call *shiksah*: blonde, tall, attractive. (His great-grandparents, who immigrated from Poland would not have thought her possible as a spouse for one of their descendants. In the Jewish Poland of "then," *shiksah* conveyed "other" and "out-of-bounds.") The first wife, later divorced, was a convert, lit Friday night candles, kept a kosher household, observed the holidays. The second wife did not and does not. He considers himself a committed and concerned, conscious Jew, contributes to the communal funds, is a strong supporter of Israel. On occasion, he attends synagogue on the major holidays, and makes an effort to observe the year of mourning and memorial days for his parents. He was actively involved in the campaign for Soviet Jewry to leave the USSR in the bad old days. What are their children?

RESIDUAL JEWISHNESS

The Yiddish-speaking Jews of Eastern Europe held that every Jew carried within him or her *a pintelle Yid*—that little "point" or kernel of Jewishness. The hasidic interpretation of the Jewish mystical text, the *Zohar*, holds that there is a spark of holiness in every Jew. But without relying on metaphysical explanations, or falling back on Jungian theory, there is something called residual Jewishness. If indeed, over 50% of the Jews marrying in the past decade have intermarried, their spouses and children may feel a residual Jewishness, even if they have not converted to Jewishness. And some of these "intermarried" and not-converted may claim Jewishness—in the Reform definition—through descent from a Jewish father.

In a revolutionary move, the Reform movement broke with the accepted norm of both Orthodox and Conservative Jewry which define a Jew as one born to a Jewish mother, whether the mother is Jewish by birth or by conversion, or one who converts. That is, the norm is *matrilinear*: in plain English "according to the line of the mother." The Reform movement adopted what is called the *patrilinear* principle: it is suficient if *either parent is Jewish.*

In other places, there is recognition of this. In Sweden, the community admits those whose descent is not—from the strict Halachic point-of-view—Jewish. But, it adds in its bylaws, that membership in the Jewish community does not necessarily mean that the member is a Jew.

According to Professor Daniel Elazar, the Reform movement's decision has led to similar, what he calls "strange situations" in the United States:*

> [Because of patrilineal descent], there is less incentive for a non-Jewish partner in a mixed marriage to convert. Before that decision, many would go through a Reform conversion for the sake of the Jewish side. Now many people raise their children in the Reform temple, claim patrilineal descent, and see no reason for conversion. . . .
>
> **In essence, the Reform movement shot itself in the foot. This has led to some very strange situations. . .** [such as in one congregation] which specifies that certain offices may be held by non-Jews, certain offices are reserved for Jews only, and the rabbi. . . must keep a register as to who is Jewish and who is not (the way the Interior Ministry does in Israel, only using a different definition).

This is a de facto accommodation, similar to the situation in Israel, yet radically different. True, people of Jewish descent may enter the country freely as immigrants entitled to citizenship—*provided they do not profess another religion, and may bring the non-Jewish members of their immediate family with them, even if the latter do profess another religion.* Similarly, the Rabbinate does not accept this as proof of Jewishness from an Halachic point-of-view. The difference though is that Israel is a state, not a community or a congregation. As a Jewish state, it has not adopted all the Halachic categories. The parallel is interesting, perhaps indicative of the future. Both Israel and the Swedish Jewish community are frameworks which wish to preserve Jewishness as an identity, without determining what their members (citizens in the

---

* "An aging, shrinking Jewry," *The Jerusalem Post*, February 26, 1991, p. 8. Emphasis added.

case of Israel) believe or practice religiously. In the case of the Reform congregation, if the same applies, we must begin to ask whether the Reform movement has a minimal credo or set of practices, or whether being a Reform Jew is simply a statement of wishing to identify with the Jewish people in some not too taxing way. The residual Jew in Israel, on the other hand, is forced by the cultural climate and lifestyle to live in a Jewish milieu and share symbols of Jewishness.

Outside of Israel, the residual Jew's identification can be aroused by a multitude of reasons. The fictional prototype is the Jew thrown out of bed by his Aryan partner when she discovers he is circumcised, the naked truth. It may go on to other, milder if less interesting manifestations of anti-Semitism, through to the need to escape active Jew-hatred or its threat, such as the present crumbling of the former Soviet Union and the dangers it presents for Jews.*

Certainly, some residual Jews have been affected—their Jewishness turned on, so to speak, when other Jews, and particularly when the State of the Jews are being attacked. Thus, for example, what the fundraisers dubbed, in the period preceding the Six-Day War and afterwards, "woodwork Jews." The phenomenon was of hundreds of "non-givers"—people unknown to the organized Jewish community—voluntarily calling, or coming in to the campaign office, to give money. To be fair, the fundraisers were not being cynical when they said, in bewilderment and even pride, "They came out of the woodwork." Behind the phenomenon, beyond the positive side, the "pintelle Yid," there is a darker resonance: the shade of the Holocaust.

Obviously, at a time when Israel was seen as in danger of receiving a death-blow, or in the case of the Scud attacks, non-Jewish spouses of mixed marriages, their offspring, and even the non-Jewish in-laws may show some sense of understanding or solidarity with Israel. So too the

---

* From the beginning of the war against Iraq, which brought Scud missile attacks on Israel, through its conclusion, a period of over five weeks, close to 13,000 new immigrants arrived in Israel. This writer was at Ben Gurion Airport on the night of January 22, 1991, and saw about 200 Soviet immigrants being briefed on the use of the gas masks they were issued immediately on arrival. Ten minutes later, in masks, we were mingling as the alarm sounded. That was the night Ramat Gan suffered dozens of casualties.

waves of immigration from Ethiopia or the CIS may stimulate residual Jews and those connected to them to raise their sense of identification with their Jewish relatives.

However, aside from the Six-Day War, when Israel removed the threat after three weeks of excruciating existential loneliness, these moments of resurgent Jewishness are passing phases, ups followed by downs, and though some individuals may become "involved" in Jewish life as a result of their making themselves known, the general trend is a drifting away. "Jews as victims" may trigger a comfortable once-in-a-while Jewishness. We do not recommend it.*

THE "POLITICAL" JEW

For some, politics has become a surrogate for national and religious identity. There are many Jews, some intermarried, who have no real connection with organized Jewish life, whether in the synagogue-temple form or that of the local federations. Yet they have a need to identify and support a central Jewish theme: Israel. They may see Israel as the last bastion of their own Jewishness, or it may be the source of pride which makes them, to their thinking, "equal" in the eyes of their non-Jewish peers.

It also provides access to important policy-makers on the American national and state political scenes, and thus enhances their own sense of Americanism. Whatever the psychology, it is a prestigious field, certainly helpful to Israel, but which also may create more ties with Jewish life. Through it, links are maintained, sometimes the children of such involved people take on their parents' interest and expand it to learning more about Judaism, or spending time in Israel on courses or tours, and thus another thread in the web of ongoing contact is spun. Once involved politically, the person will become a target for recruiters from

---

* It seems to be a cause Gentiles as well often prefer to that of a strong and capable Israel—which is no good reason for Jews and Israel to accept the role willingly. Almost all of us prefer to ensure our existence as best we can, without granting comfort to Jew or Gentile by once again being cast as victims. This is often known as "intransigence" in political elites in many countries, as well as at the United Nations.

other more identified areas of Jewish life.

Under the heading of residual, but more obviously identified Jews are *noblesse oblige* Jews. These are the "representational" families of leaders in countries where the name of the family is a living symbol of Jewry, and has been for generations. These symbolic leaders carry their Jewishness seriously and speak for the community, use their prestige and contacts behind the scenes, and often head communal and pro-Israel organizations. *Often, perhaps usually,* there is not much Jewish in their lifestyle, religious observance or marital status. In a way, they are to be admired, since they could rather easily fade away—they are often part of the ruling elite or the social in-group of their countries. *Noblesse oblige* perhaps makes them Jews, but their time, efforts and hearts are often with Jewish concerns just as other—more "naturally Jewish" Jews—who do not have the same social possibilities. Often, their Jewishness is less a delight and joy than a burden and sense of responsibility, although obviously it brings moments of pride: a member of a famous European Jewish family was seen running through the lobby of the Dan Hotel in Tel Aviv, in the fateful days of June 1967, shouting, "Nous avons gagnés, nous avons gagnés!"— We won, we won!

Yet the inroads of assimilation and loss are vast. In a 1990 demographic study of U.S. Jewry, the startling revelation was the number of non-Jews who were members of "Jewish" households. This returns us to the question of conversion, and the patrilineal issue. The Reform patrilineal decision marks a breach of Jewish custom and law observed down the generations. The innovation creates a second breach, one between it and the Orthodox and Conservatives, as well as the norm accepted in Israel not only under law, but by the vast majority of Israeli Jews.

The traditionalists within the Reform movement are restive. One highly respected Reform leader, in private conversation, critically said that his movement took a step not just affecting Reform, but affecting *Klal Yisrael.* This term, like many Hebrew terms, is fraught with associations. Klal Yisrael technically means the totality of Israel. Usually its sense is "the body of the entire Jewish people, past, present and future;" or the generality and totality of all Jews as opposed to regional, sectarian or ideological-theological differences. *In the words of this Reform leader is an unspoken fear of schism.*

A second decision by the American Reform rabbinate to open its ranks (and pulpits) to homosexuals of either gender has a similar effect. On this issue, decided in 1990, the following comment is pertinent:*

> To criticize that decision does not place one to the right of Genghis Khan or even of many Reform congregants and Rabbis. It was not an easy battle in the Reform movement. . . . the question is *not* homosexuality, nor is it the rights of homosexuals as people, citizens, or Jews. *The real question is what is a Rabbi.* In the debate, the yea-sayers fought for the right-to-employment. No decent person should limit the right of homosexuals to a job. But since when is a Rabbi just a job-holder? To be a Rabbi is a privilege, and more than that, a responsibility. No one has a "right" to be a Rabbi as one has the right to be a manager or a computer expert. That much was clear. Once the decision was taken, a lesbian rabbi triumphantly said that now she is recognized as a "role model" by her movement. If Rabbis are indeed role models, her argument provides its own response.
>
> Many of us fought on behalf of the equality of the Conservative and Reform movements on the "Who is a Jew" issue. Some of us helped these two movements receive a fair share of the Jewish Agency's budget, when they cried out against financial discrimination. Should we now have second thoughts? "Who is a Jew" assumes that there are some standards for Jewishness, and some standing for the rabbis who transform non-Jews into Jews.
>
> Second thoughts arise. If not to change sides, then to ask the Reform movement if it is really concerned with Jewish unity, and the ability of all trends in Judaism to live in a respectful and acceptable consensus. After all, perhaps (just perhaps) the Reform movement has "solved" an American problem. It has created a *Klal Yisrael*, "totality-of-Israel" problem.

---

* By this writer in a slightly different version published in *The Jerusalem Report,* November 15, 1990, p. 12.

In defense, the supporters of the patrilinear and homosexual decisions speak of the need to recognize facts, and the importance of keeping Jews within the fold: the offspring of mixed marriages, the rising number of declared homosexuals. They say that they are merely recognizing *de jure* what exists *de facto*. The synagogues had many such members who wanted to raise their children as Jews, and had in fact been permitting—actually welcoming mixed couples and their children to services and religious school. Homosexuals were already in the pulpit and if others, now able openly to reveal their sexual identity wanted to become rabbis, why not?

The critics respond that once individual issues, cared for on a one-by-one basis, become matters of principle, a breach in inter-"trend" (denomination) relations has been committed.* The Reform decision will also affect the moral pressure it can exert on the Israeli political establishment over the "Who is a Jew" issue.

The law in Israel recognizes as Jewish the child of a Jewish mother by birth or conversion, or a person converted to Judaism. The law does not specify the form of conversion, that is which rabbi of which "trend" performed the conversion. The Orthodox lobby in Israel and abroad, particularly the influential Habad hasidim (followers of the Rebbi of Lubavitch, Rabbi Schneerson) have been fighting to amend the citizenship law with the addition of two Hebrew words *lefi ha-halachah,* that is the law will recognize such conversions only if done "according to the Halachah." In effect this would delegitimize non-orthodox (i.e. Conservative and Reform) conversions.**

American liberal Jews, in either the political or religious sense see in Israel's lack of separation of (Orthodox) Synagogue and State an expression of blackest medievalism. "Who is a Jew?" is a touchstone issue

---

* Jews do not like the label "denomination" for the movements within "religious" Judaism—Orthodox, Conservative and Reform, as well as the smaller Reconstructionists. The term is felt to be Christian, and indicates a wider distance between each group than the milder "trends," which indicates that they all adhere to Klal Yisrael.

**The law relates only to what entry should be made in the citizen's identification document. Such a notation *does not bind* Israel's Rabbinic (Orthodox) courts or marriage registrars.

because it affects almost every Jewish family in North America.

"WHO IS A JEW" REVISITED

The "Who is a Jew" crisis again exploded during negotiations over forming the National Unity Government in 1988, severely scarring Israel-Diaspora relations.* It is a historic turning-point, and probably has caused irreparable harm to Israel-Diaspora relations.

This is not the first "Who is a Jew" crisis; the original cabinet crisis over the issue was in 1958. Why is 1988 so different from 1958?

Over three decades ago, the Minister of the Interior issued regulations which permitted any person who in good faith declared himself to be a Jew to be registered as such, provided that he was not a member of another religion. In other words, Orthodox practice was to be replaced by a "secular" definition. But even the "secular" definition had to use a religious criterion, at least in the negative sense, that the self-proclaimed Jew could not profess another religion. The innovation was later set aside, and a definition consonant with Orthodox practice has held sway since: a Jew is someone born to a Jewish mother or who has been converted to Judaism.

The 1988 crisis was precipitated by an Orthodox demand that conversion, to be recognized, must be "according to Halachah" (see above). In other words, the initiative—unlike 1958—came from the Orthodox side (actually the ultra-Orthodox). It was about to be embraced by the leader of the Likud—openly—and by the leader of Labor covertly to enable each side to bring the ultra-Orthodox parties into a coalition government, and thus bring either Likud or Labor into power.

The outcry against this change was so overwhelming as to force the then Prime Minister, Yitzhak Shamir, to back away from signed agreements with the Orthodox. The Deputy Prime Minister at the time, Shimon Peres had to deny that he had engaged in similar negotiations on behalf of Labor.

The Diaspora Jewish reaction was rage: in print, calls, telexes and "special missions." It embraced major bodies and leaders, especially

---

* The subject was treated by this writer in "Who is a Jew Revisited," *The Jerusalem Post,* Tuesday, December 5, 1989, p. 7.

those of the Reform and Conservative movements, but uniting as well the heads of Jewish organizations and federations, *including UJA and the Council of Federations in the United States and the Canadian United Israel Appeal.* Such open intervention by major community leaders and central fund-raising institutions was unprecedented.

Why? Jewish unity today is not a unity in strength, but a unity of weakness. The Jewish people outside of Israel is diminishing by leaps and bounds. The Zionist idea has demonstrated its weakness by not attracting Jews from affluent societies, and by serving as a second choice for Jews from lands of distress. That is a point of fact even if it contradicts the ideology or ideologies we profess. It exists regardless of assessments of Israel's diplomatic and military strength or economic resilience.

This mutual weakness creates a bonding and a sense of dependence of each partner on the other. To all that is added the importance of Israel as a rallying point for Jewish pride, and Israel's need for Diaspora Jewish political support.

In Diaspora Jewry, in the wake of the open society and a high rate of intermarriage, any Jew who feels this mutuality with Israel is threatened if Israel legislates his children or grandchildren "in" or "out" of Jewishness. Secondly, the weakness of the family and synagogue have given Israel the role of the center of Jewish identity. The overwhelming majority of Western Jews will not move their bodies to Israel, but for many part of their souls are here. Among concerned and committed Jews—the activists in the community, lobbyists, Zionist groups, federations, UJA and synagogues, the "idea" of Israel as the center and arbiter of Jewishness is powerful. It is the Zionist ideal of personal aliyah which has not been adopted.

Since Jewish identity is weakening, and Israel's role is central, and no average Diaspora family sees itself as entirely proof to mixed marriage, the constituencies then turned to the leaders. They, who face the same problem in their own families, turned in towering rage to Israel's politicians.

Emanuel Azenberg, quoted earlier, voiced this rage:

> . . . as ardent a Zionist as I am, if you don't have the strength to include me as a Jew, then I'm not coming back [to Israel] if the issue is determined by a bunch of foolish rabbis. . . .

It is amazing how the most senior level of Israeli political leadership misread the possible Diaspora Jewish reaction! In sublime assurance that Israeli political deals have nothing to do with Diaspora Jews, almost all Israeli political leaders *simply did not understand* how deeply such changes would inflame the overseas Jewish leadership.

The lack of concern of Israeli politicians multiplies the anxiety about future bouts over "Who is a Jew." Israeli political considerations may tilt the precarious status quo even further. In that case, the outlook for repairing the breach between mainstream Diaspora leaders and the leadership of the political mainstream in Israel is bleak. This is especially true as we enter upon a Diaspora third generation born after 1948, for whom the sheen of the newness of the State will take on the patina of an heirloom, treasured, taken for granted, and on rare occasion taken out of the sideboard.

CHAPTER NINE

WHO ARE THE LEADERS?[1]

Previous generations [of American Jews] have built the community buildings and institutions. That was relatively easy. They were motivated by a sense of Jewish identity that they expressed through financial generosity and an instinct that the physical manifestation of ethnic community was necessary in America. The non-Jewish neighbor had a church, we had to have a synagogue, beautiful and prominent, as proof of our existence. This generation, the fourth in America, has the hard. . . task of building systems for learning our heritage. Without this knowledge, everything our parents built will fall apart through disuse and neglect. . . . The chain of continuity begins with the parents. If they place no value on Jewish knowledge, why should their children?

—Rabbi Herbert A. Friedman

Jewish leaders appear in the Diaspora wherever Jews are organized: in synagogues, communal organizations, and Jewish politics. When Jews become prominent outside the organized Jewish world, they are seen as leaders who happen to be Jewish: their "other" identity overrides their Jewishness. Neither Leon Blum nor Pierre Mendes-France were leaders of Jews, but French political leaders who to a greater or lesser extent identified themselves as Jews. Louis Brandeis, on the other hand, was certainly in Jewish eyes a Jewish communal leader, a political Zionist; he may also have been seen this way by non-Jews. As an American, though, he was an outstanding national figure, a jurist who was a Jew.

The State of Israel created a new scale in Jewish life. Israeli political leaders became the preeminent world Jewish leaders. The more outstanding and singular the personality, the greater he or she was perceived to be. The clearest example is David Ben Gurion; but certainly Golda Meir and Menachem Begin were also seen as world Jewish leaders. The role of Prime Minister of Israel was the platform for this preeminence. However, their personality traits, charisma and public appearances earned them a place in the consciousness of the literate public across the world not merely as Jewish leaders, but as *the* Jewish leaders of the time.

State leadership has a natural advantage over communal leadership in fostering recognition and prominence. Heading a state provides immediate access to the media. Today, the telecommunications and electronic media heighten and accelerate newsmaking and open millions of homes to such coverage. In Israel's case, the newness of the state was often seen, particularly in its earlier years, as an unusual historical phenomenon, a saga of biblical proportions, both for its sources and its modern flourishing; thus it generated extensive media attention.

The phenomenon of Israeli leaders as world Jewish leaders is barely a half-century old. Traditionally, Jewish leadership has been of two types: the spiritual figure (the rabbi), and the intercessor, the political go-between or power-broker (the *shtadlan*).

In modern Jewish life, the model of the shtadlan is clearly the Rothschild family. Lord Balfour wrote his famous letter (the "Balfour Declaration," as it came to be known) of November 2, 1917 to Lord Rothschild. The Rothschild tradition is still powerful in France and, though less visibly, in Britain.

In the United States, to these two categories of leaders was added a third, which rose steadily and quietly and is now a major force to be reckoned with. The rabbis were easy to identify, as long as Jews played the role of religious (rather than ethnic or political) minority; the rabbis were the natural spokesmen. The new type of intercessors, political leaders who had an organizational base as well, included in previous generations, presidents of the American Jewish Committee — Louis Marshall and Jacob Blaustein.

But "national" leadership has evolved from the ranks of thousands of volunteer lay leaders who are not usually shtadlanim but who work quietly and effectively in social, educational, welfare, and cultural settings, often through community federations or fund-raising. Some of these eventually become national or political leaders. Thus there is a hierarchic quality to the recruitment and mobilization of leadership—quite different from the old shtadlan model. Alongside of the volunteer leader is a highly developed corps of Jewish professionals, the so-called civil servants or full-time organizational directors, who often become the power behind and, on occasion, on the throne.

The transition in the U.S. from the true shtadlan to its new version began between the World Wars. The political rabbi-leaders often competed: Stephen Wise and Abba Hillel Silver were more political than spiritual leaders, who used a "democratic" or broader, mass-organizational power base (the American Jewish Congress, the Zionist Organization of America) to challenge, in the name of democracy, the entrenched intercessor, who was often of the German-Jewish "class."

These categories do not apply to Orthodoxy proper, where leadership is attained in traditional ways. They apply to the larger community and organizational structures in the Diaspora, with varying applications, of course, from country to country.

The means of recruiting and mobilizing leaders is likewise a threefold process. Rabbis are recruited through seminaries; organizational leaders rise through the ranks of Jewish networks; professionals often pursue specialized university studies in preparation for the field.

Graduates of seminaries and rabbinical schools are usually easily placed and often at a premium. There is a blurring of lines on occasion in the case of educators who in North America are usually, but not necessarily, rabbis: they often enter communal service organizations and thus become professionals.

Not every rabbi is seen as a leader in the sense we use the term here. If the rabbi chooses to concentrate on research, study, teaching and congregational duties, he (or increasingly today, she) is in a spiritual/cultural role. Some rabbis though focus on the role of spokesperson, appearing before the media and on national organizational platforms on the other. The role of the rabbi who is a leader is not usually spiritual: he (and now she) often transfers to the organizational leadership role, even if the organization is "religious," such as a national rabbinical or synagogue organization. Their leadership then is essentially political rather than spiritual.

One must note the occasional exception, such as in the case of the late and saintly Abraham Joshua Heschel. But it is hard to separate his spiritual impact from his political involvement in such visible activities as the civil rights movement or dialogues with non-Jewish religious figures. The spiritual impact of a rabbi-leader is sometimes bolstered by his effect: veness as a fund-raiser, usually for his own synagogue, school, or educational program, occasionally for the United Jewish Appeal.

With regard to volunteer or "lay" leaders in the political sphere, leadership is achieved through a step-by-step rise through the organizational ranks, beginning with hard work and many hours on committees, organizing functions, drives, programs, and conferences. Usually, once a certain level is attained near the top, there is a built-in mechanism of advancement, selection, or election, with the most senior positions almost guaranteed. Only personal financial complications or, rarely, scandals of a business nature can halt the progression. ("Scandal" in the private life of a rising leader no longer carries the stigma it might have two generations ago; indeed, many actions are no longer considered scandalous, and may even add a certain cachet to the person in question.)

Professionals are often graduates of special programs at Brandeis University, Yeshiva University, Hebrew Union College-Los Angeles, or of studies in the field of social work and community organization. There are also cases of field promotions in which junior professionals without specific academic professional training enter the arena and their ability propels them forward. Some of these may be seminary graduates (or drop-outs), educators, would-be businessmen, or those who entered the Jewish scene after spending time in Israel and, though not prepared to live there, were bitten by the Zionist bug. Thus Israeli academia, especially the Hebrew University, must be added to the list of sources for recruitment, particularly in North America. In other countries, Jewish and Zionist youth movements often produce professionals as a by-product of their work.

In the past decade or so, a new phenomenon has swept across North America, perhaps as a modern version of the old *maggidim*, the spell-binding, often itinerant synagogue preachers. For want of a better term, "guru" best describes it. They are the new maggidim, the moral teachers and preachers. Today they are booked through their own seminar organizations, or on contract to national organizations and lecture circuits; they attend week-end seminars and lectures at various gatherings. Their popularity waxes and wanes according to the laws of exposure and over-exposure, fame and notoriety, fads and fees. Because they have a grassroots appeal born of charisma and message, their impact lies outside organizational structures, and therefore makes them the exception to the three categories of leadership laid out above.

Certainly, in modern times, leadership is highly dependent on the communications media. The press has been reinforced, if not supplanted, by the electronic media. Exposure is purchased by costly public relations experts; issues can unfortunately deteriorate into mere media events or "photo opportunities"; and often the name of the game is capturing another media personality to appear next to on the podium. Thus the President of the United States, famous public servants or officials, authors and TV or film personalities not only attract the crowd, but by a process of sharing the mantle confer some of their charisma onto the Jewish leader. This is a common denominator in organized Jewish life today and, in the opinion of some, a low one. Israel has lent itself to this, with unexpected results. The inflation of media exposure by its leading public figures has often led to a deflation in their prestige.

The scope of a leader's following depends upon his access to media: local, regional, national, and international. Israeli figures garner wide attention. Similarly, Jewish Diaspora figures who take sides on international issues involving state leaders enjoy unwonted publicity. Two cases in point are the Bitburg and the Waldheim affairs. (The Bitburg affair flared when then-President Ronald Reagan was to make an official trip to Germany, including a war cemetery in which SS soldiers were buried. Kurt Waldheim's nomination and election to the Presidency of Austria after hiding his type of service and behavior in the German army in World War II was another *cause celebre*.)

The power of the media leads to considerable competition among leaders, particularly in the United States. In addition to their public relations apparatuses and conferences held with the media in mind, sometimes the principals themselves cultivate close ties with journalists, just as politicians.

Wealth is a great advantage in this pursuit of leadership. Wealthy men and women may sometimes reach the stage where their affairs require less time, effort, and attention or, on the other hand, no longer offer a challenge. Public service is then not only available, it fairly beckons, since every organization seeks persons of wealth, which is equated with stature and prestige. Often, such men, and increasingly women, are also coveted for their ability to recruit peers, or to solicit funds from them. And finally, the leader's own financial contribution can be an important boon for the organization's income.

Indeed, often it seems that campaign leaders of a certain type see their involvement with their organization and campaign as a consuming hobby. In the pragmatic, competitive and result-oriented business world in which they live, "the bottom line" is, of course, the ultimate measuring-rod of success. This is sometimes, possibly often transferred over to the campaign. "So-and-so raised X million last year. This year, we (read 'I') plan to raise X+ million."

This is part of the general American—or is it Western?—milieu. The former U.S. Secretary of State, James Baker, described himself in these words: "I'm more interested in the contest than the philosophy. Once I'm in the contest, bang! That's it." The interviewer added about Baker: Most issues, he says, interest him only as potential victories to be won or embarrassing losses to be avoided.*

Sometimes then, the means become an end in themselves. The ideological position is mushy, sentimental, or unarticulated. That is not to gainsay the true devotion of the armies of volunteers or to tar all leaders with that brush. But there is too much of the other, the "let's show 'em" syndrome. Another face of this, perhaps more typical of the older generation, is the statement made in pride, "Israel is 'my country club.'" What the speaker means, of course, is that he devotes all his non-business time to Israeli causes, just as others find their leisure (hobby?) on the golf course or at the card table of a country club. For those to whom Israel represents blood and sweat, the statement is condescending.

If, ideally, the Jewish aristocracy of the past was the aristocracy of learning, it has become evident more and more throughout this century (though it was undoubtedly true to some extent in previous ages) that "money talks." Men of substance are most comfortable with men of substance; "money talks to money." "Spiritual" leaders are often referred to as "*my* rabbi"—with the stress on the possessive. *The aristocracy of learning yields to the plutocracy of wealth.*

---

* William A. Henry III, "Positively Republican," *American Way*, vol. 22, No. 2, January 15, 1989, p. 28.

On the other hand, competition and the need to ensure widespread support and viability of candidates within the leadership network demand rotation in leadership positions; the hope of advancement and the assurance of turn-over in theory ensures accountability and responsible leadership. Many leaders come to organized Jewish life in middle age, from vastly different backgrounds. They land in a field whose complexities are many: religious and ideological shadings and outright differences within movements; historic postures on Zionism, anti-Zionism and non-Zionism; local versus national or international Jewish interests; the political party identification or allegiance of the individual leader versus the overall community interest; pro- and anti-Jewish education; defining financial priorities in federations or other organizations; personal rivalries. . . . The list is inexhaustible.

Thus the professional Jewish leader, sitting astride the intricacies of Jewish life, takes on greater power as the guardian of the past, the recorder and walking reminder of history, recent or less recent. He is familiar with the subtleties, the foibles, the pet peeves and preferences of competing leaders or organizations; he has media awareness and contacts, besides the normal and obvious organizational skills he has or is presumed to have. The rotation of volunteer leadership, though hardly invented by the professionals, makes the professional into a mandarin class. This is bolstered by high salary standards in North America, both as a way of keeping "good" men and women in the fold of Jewish life, and as a symbol of prestige and power for the individual professional and his organization. "If he gets that much, he must be worth it."

Usually the lay leaders and professionals work well together, and rise above personality and policy differences. Occasionally confrontation arises between a professional and a lay leader jealous of or unbeholden to the established powerful professional. The battle usually concludes with the professional being gracefully — and generously — retired and replaced with a more compatible or complaisant successor.

Plutocracy and professionalization in Jewish life are effects of the Jewish "poverty" of those who become Jewish leaders. Some decades ago, the late Dr. Israel Goldstein had the courage to say:

> Wanted—an educated Jewish laity! Perhaps it is too much to expect Jewish laymen in America to possess the degree of

learning which used to be prevalent among Jewish laymen in the Old World; but for all that, the prevailing condition of *am ha-aratzut* [ignorance] must not be tolerated. . . . Jewish life in America has become cheap and vulgar, for the lack of a broader base of educated Jewish laity. A thousand educated Jewish laymen in a community of ten thousand Jews would create an atmosphere in which Jewish scholarship would flourish because it would be respected, in which Jewish books would have a market, in which Jewish education would receive at least as much attention as Jewish philanthropy, and in which assurance instead of alarm would be the leitmotif.*

These words are as apt today as when penned. There has been some improvement in the quality of Jewish education, background, and involvement of younger leaders. This stems in part from wider day-school enrollment and religious summer camp activities, and in part from leadership programs or informal or formal study periods in Israel, which foster greater awareness of Jewish complexities and Israeli realities.

Leadership training has been fostered by UJA and Federation Young Leadership, the Wexner Heritage Foundation and Clal as well as similar programs. There is a growing trend, especially in North America, to institute study programs in local federation leadership groups, often with the help of outside consultants.

But such trends notwithstanding, how many Jewish leaders know the names of the biblical books or can provide a periodization of Jewish history or a sketch of its key figures through the ages? How many read or speak Hebrew with any fluency, or use Jewish criteria, Halachic or biblical, to analyze problems and seek solutions? Israel itself is too often seen through a muddle of slogans and sentimentalities as a poor, benighted cousin who must be helped as a mitzvah; there is little desire really to know Israel, to live there for extended periods (short of aliyah), and little encouragement of children to do so.

In spite of the few seminary graduates who maintain standards of Jewish scholarship and despite the mushrooming of Jewish studies

---

* *Jewish Perspectives: Selected Addresses, Sermons, and Articles, 1915–1983,* Jerusalem, Keter Publishing House, pp. 140–41.

departments in hundreds of universities throughout the world, the face of the lay leadership is also the face of the professionals. Does the job description for any major executive in the most important Jewish communities and national or international Jewish organizations require an extensive background in Jewish classics, Hebrew, religion, or history?

Furthermore, in the free enterprise tradition of North America, and the overwhelming and blessed voluntarism which characterizes Jewish life, there exists a multiplicity of organizational structures. The Conference of Presidents of Major Jewish Organizations in the U.S. consists of dozens of constituent bodies, many overlapping, all competing for budgets and media attention, prestige and prominence. Other major Jewish organizations exist that are prevented from joining for legal or tax reasons. This multiplicity leads to an avoidance or obfuscation of basic Jewish sociological, ideological, or religious problems. The competition makes the establishment of standards for leadership difficult, if not impossible.

The strictly Orthodox world has its own charismatic leadership; but many of these leaders do not wish to be, nor are they necessarily equipped or trained to be leaders of all Jews, including the non-Orthodox. Thus the state of "general" Jewish leadership in the Diaspora is, as we have seen, far from desirable. Is this sad state immutable? The solution may sound utopian, but without utopian aims, what would we be?

First, rabbis and knowledgeable lay leaders should continue to propagate the idea that Jewish leaders must be Jewishly trained and educated. That this requires both civic courage and the risk of unpopularity does not absolve anyone of the responsibility. Second, major national and international organizations must put the issue higher on their agendas. Special seminars, "retreats," and widely publicized national and international conferences specifically devoted to this issue should be organized. Third, established leaders should be encouraged to undertake private or group study programs. (Both the Wexner Heritage Foundation and Clal are already doing this on a limited basis in the U.S., as is Melitz in Israel.)

This may seem far-fetched, but actually it might be the very idea the younger and better-educated elements might choose as the battle cry and instrument for advancement. Given as well the penchant of large organizations to borrow liberally from the platforms of their competitors, and their need for "programming," the vitality of the idea becomes evident. The younger elements might very well find comfort from those professionals who do have the appropriate education, and are secure in their leadership. Ideas have a way of percolating. And finally, it requires a few courageous lay leaders who are willing not only to sponsor education, as fortunately many are, but who are willing to engage in self-education, who could serve as role models.

The need for educated Jewish leaders must also be seen against the wider background. We have shown that there is a growing gap between Israeli and Diaspora perceptions of Judaism and Jewishness. Though the average Israeli cannot claim any great familiarity with Talmudic sources or Halachic interpretations, there are nevertheless at least four factors which contribute to some familiarity with Judaic life and lore: the presence of graduates of *yeshivot* — Talmudical academies — and of religious schools in the civil service and body politic; a growing demand to upgrade Jewish studies in the school system; and the nature of Israel's calendar and legal system, which shape daily life and create some form of osmosis between the people and key facets of tradition and even Halachah, and, perhaps most important, the Hebrew language, which permits access to texts and provides a rich associative frame of reference.

Despite the basic experiential differences between the Diaspora and Israel, the rift can be mitigated to some extent by Judaic knowledge, study of Bible, and the learning of Hebrew. This approach can supply an ideological underpinning and justification for the proposals or ideas expressed above. Israel should be a major resource for this process: the site of retreats, seminars, study programs and enrichment exercises.

The growing receptivity to Jewish education, both in the national and world Jewish community should present a new opportunity: to concentrate on the individual within this general trend. If leaders adopt slogans of change, they may begin to act on them. If they do not, perhaps their followers will compel them to implement the messages they proclaim.

Israel does not lack for "leaders," that is people in roles of political and economic leadership who usually have much better Jewish backgrounds than their Diaspora counterparts. It does not necessarily make them better leaders. In addition, their general Jewish knowledge often does not embrace deep and serious knowledge of the Jewish condition in the Diaspora, another lack which could be corrected by changes in the educational system.

Our concern here, though, is not with the quality of leaders *qua* leaders, but the Jewish dimension which can create a common language of shared symbols and associations to keep this dispersed and riven people united. The leaders, however defined, without that common language, that shared universe of discourse, may unwittingly simply lead to greater division and deeper rifts.

Since Mishnaic times, Jewish learning has been compulsory and widely embraced. Emancipation, civic freedom in Diaspora societies, and generations of cultural drift have created their own dynamic, undermining and destroying the basis of collective, family and individual Jewish life. If Jewish leaders do not lead the Jews back to a cohesiveness and encourage Jewish knowledge, who will? And if they do not, whom will they have to lead?

---

1. This chapter was originally written while the author was engaged in thinking through the premises of this book. It appeared in different forms in a *Festschrift* in honor of Rabbi Leon Kronish as well as in *Midstream*. See Avraham Avi-hai, "Leadership" in *Towards The Twenty-First Century: Judaism and the Jewish People In Israel and America. Essays in honor of Rabbi Leon Kronish on the Occasion of his Seventieth Birthday.* Ronald Kronish, ed. Hoboken, Ktav, 1988. Also *Midstream*, May 1988.

This version opens with a citation from Rabbi Herbert Friedman, who was Executive Chairman of the UJA for about two decades from 1956. He created a UJA Young Leadership Division, whose "graduates" may be found at top levels of organized American Jewish life. He is President of the Leslie Wexner Heritage Foundation. The quotation, from *Moment*, December 1990 was reproduced in *The Jerusalem Post*, December 18, 1990, p. 8.

CHAPTER TEN

THE "TORAH CAMP": THE ULTRA-ORTHODOX

The rifts within the ultra-Orthodox (*haredi*) communities are deep, the differences between ultra-Orthodox groups are so profound. Can they be considered as one group, let alone one possible evolving Jewish people? In spite of conflict and great diversity, the ultra-Orthodox share basic elements of a common lifestyle and belief system. The similarities among the ultra-Orthodox are greater than the differences. Below are basic concepts they share.

EMUNAT HACHAMIM

This phrase means belief in the wise (*Hachamim* = rabbis in this context). This is the root: faith that the transmitted or "Oral" Law, its interpretation, and decisions of Halachah as laid down by the rabbis from the time of the Mishnah until today are binding, that they are the true and authoritative determination of God's will as given to Moses. This faith does not merely apply to "ritual" in the synagogue or occasional religious observances in the home but to all facets of life.

The *Shulchan Aruch* [The Prepared or Set Table] is the codex of Jewish Law which details how one should rise in the morning, wash one's hands, pray, and continues with minutiae of behavior in all fields until one recites the prayer celebrating the One and Sole God

---

* *Haredi* is the current Hebrew term for ultra-Orthodox; *dati* is reserved for the modern Orthodox.

on going to bed.* It covers every aspect of human behavior.

The Shulchan Aruch deals with belief and faith, love, sex, marriage and child-rearing, studies, business rules and behavior, human relations, food, birth and death, charity, dress, home and synagogue rituals, prayer. It is total; it is all-embracing, a guide which, once internalized through study, repetition, and the force of example has an indelible quality which stamps the Orthodox and certainly the ultra-Orthodox from the inside out.

Thus, for example, even a discussion of the separation of religion and politics does not make sense in this context, since the one exists merely to serve the other, and a state which does not actively assist the religion to flourish is of no use to the Halachah. Ironically, therefore, the *haredi* parties believe that in a state such as Israel, religion must receive state support but not interference; they may be part of the system or at least partake of its fruits as long as their way of life is untouched.

Differences in religious practice among groups within ultra-Orthodoxy and Orthodoxy stem from differing interpretations or rulings by varying rabbinic decisors. To the outsider, these really do not seem to be very great: the order in which prayers should be recited; or which rabbinic authority's ruling on *Kashrut* should be followed. The minutiae of observance often becomes an end in itself: the stricter the better.

Indeed, it is this anxiety to be the most observant or "strictest" decisor of Law which marks ultra-Orthodoxy today, and which in recent decades has increasingly influenced the modern Orthodox. Some of the great rabbis of the past were those who found ways to be lenient. The leaders of today's ultra-Orthodox feel the need to erect greater "fences" around the Law and demand ever greater adherence to the small print of the Halachah. Why?

The Emancipation confronted traditional Judaism with a dilemma: enjoying the riches of Western civilization would invariably mean weakening the communal structure which had preserved Judaism in dispersion among the nations. Some, such as Moses Mendelssohn and

---

* The *Shulchan Aruch* was first published by Rabbi Yosef Karo in 1565. The modified Ashkenazi version was produced by Rabbi Moshe Isserles of Krakow in 1569–71. A short version, *Kitzur Shulchan Aruch* [The Abbreviated "Set table"] was written by one of the sterner decisors, Rabbi Shlomo Ganzfried in 1864, and is to be found in most Orthodox homes.

Samson Raphael Hirsch in Germany, sought ways to synthesize the two or at least defuse the danger by combining the modern lifestyle with the principles and practices of the Halachah. Others, however, were less optimistic. In their eyes, the temptations of modern society would invariably draw Jews away from the law and therefore from Judaism, as indeed often occurred. Consequently, it was essential to turn away from modernity and huddle next to a wall until the storm passed.

The practical meaning of this is clear to anyone who has walked through Williamsburg or Meah Shearim: ultra-Orthodox Jews dress differently than the rest of Jewish — even Orthodox — society, and if they are Ashkenazim, speak a different language, Yiddish.[1] Most try to keep contact with the outside world to a bare minimum. Those who point out the absurdity of Jews claiming to be more "religious" by wearing the Polish garb of the 18th century miss the point, which is to provide another bulwark of separation, a uniform which is unmistakable. It will not permit its wearer to enter "forbidden" places, it imposes upon him a discipline and mode of behavior, and it enshrines the principle of opposing change.[2]

There is a fascinating sociology of dress in the ultra-Orthodox and Orthodox communities, which makes a statement to the trained eye: type of *shtreimel* (fur cap); type of hat, size of brim, where worn on the head (slanted forward or tilting back); size and color of *kippa*, and whether knitted, cloth or velvet; *peyot* (sidelocks) and whether worn dangling, curled, tucked behind the ear or tied together under the kippa; beard, cut, untrimmed, or never trimmed and wound up to be tucked under the chin; *tzitzit* (ritual fringes), worn over shirt, or only fringes showing, or beneath the outer clothing and not visible, wool or cotton; type and color of Shabbat garment, colored, striped, material, length, cut, buttoned left or right, no jacket, tie, no tie, open collar; color of socks, how worn: over trousers (breeches) or below trousers.

For women, there are similar categories especially dealing with head-coverings, shaven or unshaven heads, type of wig, no wig, cloth cover: how far down on forehead: showing no hair, some hair, or showing a peek at the wig; "alluring" wigs and modest wigs; make-up or none; color of clothing, type of stockings; length of skirt, length of sleeves, and so on. Thus, that which separates Jews from the rest of the world is helpful in the preservation of Judaism, the logic goes, and therefore is required. It is this feeling of being under siege and assuming an active defense against the enlightenment which creates the sense of coherence in the ultra-Orthodox camp, a mirror-image of the secular sense of being under siege by the ultra-Orthodox.

There are limits, however, to the separation. Ultra-Orthodox leaders are quite naturally unwilling to cut off their noses to spite their faces, and do take from the outside world what they can. The "outside world" includes the State of Israel. From an ideological point of view, the ultra-Orthodox do not consider Israel as much better and, in a sense, actually worse than any non-Jewish government. If one may tap resources in a Diaspora country, why not Israel? (The exception is the few hundred families of Netorei Karta and the more numerous but as virulently anti-Zionist Satmar hasidim, who will accept nothing from the State.) Thus government funding for yeshivot and other institutions, grants for men who study instead of working, and other basic public services are anxiously sought by the community to foster its growth. In fact, it was this rationalization which led the ultra-Orthodox political parties to become involved in Israeli politics.

On the surface this approach seems grasping and selfish — to take from the state without giving back, but several caveats need to be emphasized. First of all, politics is about power and budgets, and if the other parties (starting with Ben Gurion's Labor movement) were willing to accept such arrangements for their own political purposes, one can hardly blame the ultra-Orthodox. Indeed, the latter have often claimed that the flow of funds and entitlement to their communities is no different in principle than that to the kibbutzim, obtained by the politicians in the agricultural lobby.*

Secondly, the ultra-Orthodox or *haredim* do make up a significant percentage of the Israeli population, and therefore are entitled to the benefits of citizenship. Just as representatives of ultra-Orthodox neighborhoods in North America are expected to tend to their needs, so too Members of Knesset should be there to represent the haredi voters.

Finally, and perhaps most important, the ultra-Orthodox see their lifestyle and principles as infinitely important to the Jewish people than

---

* The secular retort, of course, is that the kibbutzim are productive segments of society which benefit the state, and that their cemeteries show how many kibbutz members were killed in battle.

that of the non-Orthodox. In their view of the world and Western society, the haredim see themselves as the vanguard of the Jewish people, ensuring its survival, both spiritually and physically. Thus they seriously advance the claim that their studies in yeshivot are as vital to the state as service in the army. At the same time, therefore, the ultra-Orthodox can condemn the idea of the Jewish State and insist that only they are keeping it Jewish. More contact with Israeli society and the army would, the argument continues, contaminate the traditional way of life and carry the seeds of a worse disaster than those Jews have already experienced.

TALMUD TORAH

Literally, study of the Torah, it is considered so important that the tradition equates it with all the other mitzvot. This statement is included in the Morning Prayer service, so that every Jew who uses the traditional *siddur* or prayer-book, recites it daily.* If *Emunat Hachamim* ensures mores and behavior, *Talmud Torah* ensures the content: for that end — study — Jews live.

The centers of Torah study, the heartland of world Orthodoxy and ultra-Orthodoxy were all but wiped out in Europe. Wondrously, it has risen from its ashes. Never in Jewish history, we are told, have so many Torah students been amassed as in Israel today. The rebirth began with education. Today's ultra-Orthodox school systems sponsored by the various sub-groups share one basic characteristic: Torah study as the core and base of the curriculum.

Thus, in their elementary schools — with some notable, but few exceptions — varying levels of basics are taught: grammar, history, or science. But in some, only arithmetic is included. The main stress is on Pentateuch, Mishnah, Shulchan Aruch and Gemara (the Five Books of Moses, religious laws and customs, and Talmud, including as many commentators and exegetes as possible.) Even the Prophets are usually neglected. There is no standard curriculum, though, and each sub-system

---

* Mishnah *Peah*, 81, beginning, "These are the commandments which have no predetermined limits. . . " That is, one can do as much as one chooses. It ends, *Ve-talmud Torah ke-neged kullam*: but the study of the Torah is equal to them all."

follows its own emphases. The language of instruction can be Yiddish or Hebrew; the Yiddish is often a signpost of how far right the yeshiva or elementary school is placed.

These school systems employ large staffs of administrators and teachers, thus creating a vital economic nexus between the supporter-employee and the system which employs him or her. In this context, a new force has entered the field: *Shas*, an ultra-Orthodox Sephardi party. There has been a veritable explosion in the area of Sephardi ultra-Orthodox education in the latter part of the 1980s. Due to the power of the swing vote of Shas in the coalition, and the desire of both Labor and Likud to court the good-will and support of Shas, massive funding has been directed to its new school system.

THE ROLE OF THE WOMAN AND FAMILY

The ultra-Orthodox system requires the woman to fill the elemental role of nourisher, child-bearer, and quite usually to be the main bread-winner. The view from the secular world that ultra-Orthodox women are oppressed is ridiculed in haredi circles. The woman, in their view, is respected because of her God-given role. It is she who keeps the family running and ensures the Jewishness of the home, not to mention the all-important job (mitzvah) of bearing children. Thus, aside from the respect Orthodox practice demands of husband and children for the mother, her influence in the family is great.

Viewed from the outside, the child-bearing role seems overwhelming. Young women of 25, who seem much older and care-worn, are already mothers of six or seven children. For the community, the children count, and are counted. Demography, or the applied demography of the ballot box, seems to support the notion that haredim are, numerically, the wave of the future. There are now an estimated 270,000 to 300,000 haredim in Israel out of a Jewish population of over four million. There were only a handful in the country when it became an independent state with a Jewish population of approximately 600,000. Within the haredi community, an astonishing 40% are under the age of six and nearly 60% are under the age of 25.

THE MEN: A LEGION OF PERPETUAL STUDENTS

Soon after the establishment of the State, Israel's first Prime Minister,

David Ben Gurion made a concession to the reigning Torah scholar of the day, Rabbi Abraham Yeshayahu Karelitz, (known as the *Hazon Ish*, the title of one his books), agreeing to defer the mobilization of yeshiva students from military service. These were to replace the scholars lost to the Jewish people in the Holocaust. At first this affected only 400 exceptionally gifted yeshiva students. Over the years their numbers grew steadily both in absolute terms and as a proportion of the total intake of draftees. Today an estimated 20,000 ultra-Orthodox males enjoy deferments which in effect exempt them from service. The number is equivalent to two-and-a-half Israeli divisions. This means that one in fifteen potential conscripts does not serve at all or serves a limited period after the age of 25-30.*

These men enjoy the privilege of learning due not only to grants, but because of the readiness of their wives to work and help support the family. Some may see it is a sacrifice, but almost all would deem it worthwhile. To a great extent the foundation of women's schools and teachers' seminaries patterned on the Beit Ya'acov system made this possible. Micha Odenheimer wrote:

> Women who had been educated in the Beit Ya'acov schools and teachers' seminaries were no longer torn between staying at home and working "out there," where they would be exposed to the modern world. By working as teachers within the system of haredi elementary and high schools that was quickly developing in Israel, they could help support their families while remaining within an environment that recognized and affirmed their values.
>
> It soon became apparent that, if they were willing, they could play a heroic part in that world. They could take upon themselves a major part of the financial burden of supporting their fast growing families, freeing their husbands to devote

---

* Orthodox women, it may be recalled, are exempt upon presenting proof of Orthodoxy. This does not prevent modern Orthodox women from opting to serve as soldiers or in an alternate national service, for example, as teachers or nurses' aides. The ultra-Orthodox oppose service for all women — observant or not.

themselves full time — at least for the first few years of marriage — to the study of Torah, the ultimate value and ideal of
haredi life. Thousands have streamed into the institute called
the *kollel*.*

The *kollel* is an advanced institution for Talmud studies in which
married "graduate students" of yeshivot can continue full-time, or almost full-time studies. The students receive grants to study there, and
some register in morning, afternoon or evening kollelim and thus
receive a reasonable income. The early modern kollelim, modelled on
the first one probably established by Rabbi Yisrael Lipkin of Salant,
Lithuania (Reb Yisrael Salanter) in the 1880s, posited that the brightest
students, the *il'uim* should spend years of study before going out into the
world. Today's kollelim serve parts of an entire generation, helped
along by deferral of military service, government grants and contribu-
tions. Their large numbers create resentment, since thousands of young
men are not otherwise gainfully employed, leading to charges of
parasitism.

Young haredi men are actively encouraged by their society to evade
army service because it is the great socializing melting pot, "the fiery
passageway into [secular] Zionist society." Leaders of the haredim fear
that a young man, having crossed through this passageway, is lost to his
community forever. The irony here is that ghetto walls pulled down by
the Emancipation in Europe have been shored up in modern Israel.

BA'ALEI TESHUVAH: "RETURNEES" TO ORTHODOXY

There are indeed some Jews who "return" and become observant
modern Orthodox. However, the phenomenon is mainly that of joining
one of the ultra-Orthodox groups. Young secular Jews have been at-
tracted to yeshivot set up for "born-again" Ba'alei Teshuvah. Indeed,
some refer to these yeshivot as the Ba'al Teshuvah industry.

Many new yeshivot, almost all ultra-Orthodox, have been established to cater to the needs of "converts:" secular young Israelis after
army service, and university dropouts and graduates from the Diaspora.

---

* Odenheimer and Friedman quotes, *The Jerusalem Post* International edition,
  week ending January 14, 1989.

The yeshivot use talented, often charismatic figures, who seek out lonely souls at the *Kotel* (the Western Wall), or who advertise free or cheap hostels and food, usually in the Old City to attract potentials. Some yeshivot have established counterpart programs for women. The institutions have often been given access to secular schools or military bases, where well-meaning educators or officers, concerned about their charges' ignorance of the tradition have invited them in for study days or lectures.*

In her book on the Ba'alei Teshuvah, Dr. Janet Aviad stated that the modern Orthodox object to the anti-Zionist cast imparted to the undiscriminating "newly Jewish" students.** The ultra-Orthodox yeshivot catering to Westerners, some of which have opened branches abroad, carefully disguise their anti-Zionism, as will be seen in another chapter. For example, a Toronto Jew who was asked by one returnee yeshivah, Aish Ha-Torah to make a donation, said he would do so only if the institution were Zionist. He was told it would not "officially" admit to this.

An Orthodox critic of the Ba'al Teshuvah movement — himself quite close to the haredi community — did not spare his lash from what he called "the dependency" the movement fosters. "After two or three years of 'returning' them, and having them study in immersion courses, they should be encouraged to enter the normal (ultra-Orthodox) world. But they never let go. How long will they be Ba'alei Teshuvah? When do they become like everyone else in our community?"

Still, almost all ultra-Orthodox and many modern Orthodox Jews treat the Ba'al Teshuvah as a symbolic figure and relate to him within their own historical perspective as follows: the twentieth century threatened the continuity of Judaism. First the Nazis murdered six million, demolishing the major centers of Torah study. And the victory of Zionism presented the danger that its secularism would wean faithful

---

* The backlash against "those who return" has created a minor counter-phenomenon called "those who question": *ba'alei she-elah*. The Hebrew terms have a symmetry lacking in English. As a result of this group's criticism of permitting "proselytizing" by ultra-Orthodox representatives in military bases, access by them to army units has been limited if not completely forbidden.

** Janet Aviad, *A Return to Judaism*, Chicago, University of Chicago Press, 1983.

Jews away from Orthodox observance. Thus, in both Zionist and non-Zionist Orthodox communities, the teshuvah phenomenon is viewed as one of the signs of an impending and inevitable triumph over secular culture.

THE ATTRACTION OF ULTRA-ORTHODOXY

To an outsider the ultra-Orthodox world seems a closed phalanx or even an enigma. To the secular Israeli, often it is an object of hatred, dislike, ideological rivalry, or at best an uncomfortable reminder of the ghetto life Israel came to overthrow. To the American, still further removed from it, it seems light years away.

What then is the power and attraction of its lifestyle? What does the ultra-Orthodox world give its adherents? It gives them a sure path on which to tread, a sheltered society both for the spiritual and material needs, an immense closed support system with a structured and hierarchic solidarity. It offers joyous holidays and feasts, frequent family celebrations, a sense of historic continuity and chosenness. For many, it proffers reliance on Providence to supply the necessities of life without all the responsibilities and burdens that other Israelis carry.

This of course sounds idyllic. It ignores the stresses, neuroticism, family problems, financial struggles, psychological break-downs, and the tug-of-war between the sacred and the profane. But in the best of cases, the idyll described above is accurate for many, or at least so they would wish to perceive their reality. And for some it does indeed exist so. For the secular, obviously, every positive point can be seen as a negative.

THE SUPPORT SYSTEM

The ultra-Orthodox world, especially in its major strong-holds: Jerusalem and Bnei Brak in Israel, Williamsburg, Boro Park and the Orthodox enclaves in Rockland County, and Lakewood, New Jersey, provide a womb-to-tomb cocoon. In Israel, the various communities provide health care, (sometimes even special health insurance), maternity rest homes, schools, summer camps or vacation activities. They also operate special low-cost supermarkets, personal as well as institutional social welfare services, a vast circle of free-loan societies, stipends for adult students, housing projects, and an effective lobby to receive government benefits in the form of child bonuses, housing loans, and exemption from military service. The list is not complete. There is an element of personal concern, of caring.

An ultra-Orthodox woman who had been one of the first teachers in a Ba'al Teshuvah school for women contracted a fatal illness. Within hours a world-wide telephone chain was established to recite Psalms for her recovery.

Ultra-Orthodox hospitals exist in a number of centers. All Israeli hospitals are kosher, observe the Sabbath in the public areas and do not operate or do tests on the Sabbath, but for emergencies. They have special separations between the morgue and the rest of building, so that *Kohanim* (members of families descended from the priestly class, who observe certain prohibitions such as not being under the same roof as a corpse) may enter the building. Notwithstanding all of these rules, for the ultra-Orthodox the "ordinary" hospitals do not ensure strict enough compliance with the Halachah; only "special" hospitals are considered religiously acceptable.

In Jerusalem, for example, Shaarei Tzedek hospital has always been especially regarded by the ultra community, as is Bikur Holim Hospital: on the Sabbath, entries in medical reports, admissions, etc. are made by non-Jews — *Shabbes-goyim* in traditional parlance. The hasidic sect of Zanz established Laniado Hospital in Netanya. Now a new ultra-Orthodox medical center has opened in the Bnei Brak area. In writing about the new ultra-Orthodox hospital in Bnei Brak, the afternoon daily *Yediot Aharonot* called it another block in the bulwark of separation.

The walls go higher. Haredi society seems hermetically sealed and permanently secure.* However, Professor Menachem Friedman, a sociologist at Bar Ilan University notes that their very success may boomerang.

> Haredi society is based upon a rejection of modernity and its values. . . on the desire to isolate itself from the influence of the modern world. Yet economically, unlike the Amish in

---

* Odenheimer and Friedman quotes, *The Jerusalem Post* International edition, week ending January 14, 1989.

America, for example, the haredim are totally dependent on the very world they are trying to reject.

Micha Odenheimer writes in *The Jerusalem Post*:

This explosion of children and young people is without doubt, a tribute to the enormous success the haredi community has had in raising a generation committed to their parents' values. Yet this very success may be the cause of radical change. According to sociologists and demographers who study this community, haredi population growth may very soon lead to situations that could shake the institutions and structure of the haredi way of life to the very core.

---

1. The early sources attribute Israel's redemption from Egypt, among other reasons, to the fact that they did not change their names (i.e., did not adopt "foreign"— Egyptian — names), and did not change their language. This tradition dates back to the third century, and shows that assimilation was then a problem. One source may be found in *Mekhilta de-Rabbi Yishmael*, Massekhet de Pascha, Pareshah Heh, p. 14, critical edition, Horowitz–Rabin. The detective work on these sources was done by Joshua Levinson, whom I thank.

Yisrael Weinberg continued the search for "they did not change their mode of dress." In the *Haggadah shel Pesach* edited by Reuven Margoliyot (Tel Aviv, Zohar, n.d.), there is a commentary on the Haggadah's statement that the children of Israel "stood out" (*b'nei Yisrael hayu metzuyanim sham*) in Egypt, that is they were obviously different from the Egyptians. Margoliyot refers the reader to *Pesikta de-Rav Kahana*, an early compendium of *Midrash*, on *Beshalach* (the synagogue reading from *Exodus* 10:17 through 17:16). There, four reasons are given for the Israelites redemption from Egypt; four ways that the Jews did not assimilate to the Egyptian way of life: by not changing their names, their language, not engaging in gossip, and avoiding sexual promiscuity. Then Margoliyot adds a note that usually one of these four is recalled as "not changing their ways of dress." He too could find no source for this, but it is usually accepted as part of what may be called preventive medicine against assimilation.

2. The *Shulchan Aruch* states that on awakening, one should wash away the night's impurities from the fingertips before saying the first prayer, expressing thanks for the restoration of the soul. The usual practice is to set a cup of water and basin next to one's bed. In Yiddish, this is called *Negelvasser* —literally "nailwater"— water for washing the fingertips. A rabbi of the last century, when consulted by a community on what to look for in candidates for their local rabbinate, was expected to say: Seek great wisdom, or superior learning, or a good name. Instead he said, "Make sure he practices *Negelvasser*." This must be seen on the background of the principle that innovation is prohibited by the Torah: if the rabbi is not influenced by change, he can be counted upon to be careful and precise in every detail!

CHAPTER ELEVEN

SECULARIZING INFLUENCES

In the Diaspora, the ultra-Orthodox can create walls to separate themselves from the gentile world, cross those walls when convenient and then retreat behind them again. They can even separate themselves most of the time from other Jews, again when this is convenient, by lumping them with non-Jews: that is, the "others" are Jews who have adopted non-Jewish ways.

In Israel, this separation is not as easy as it looks. The society of reference is Jewish. The language is Hebrew. The holidays/holy days are Jewish. All these add up to a challenge. This explains the disdain, the hostility, even the hatred that characterizes relations between some parts of the ultra-Orthodox community and many Israelis. It is sibling hatred to the nth degree. Among other things, it underlies ultra-Orthodoxy's rejection of the civil religion. This ranges from burning the Israeli flag on Yom Ha-Atzma'ut to studied indifference.

However, there must be some seepage from the "outside" into the life of the ultra-Orthodox communities of the Diaspora. This can only be more pronounced in Israel. Proximity, blood relationships, mutual dependence and preservation of life all have a telling effect.

A conversation with a six-year old child shortly after the Six-Day War. Speaking in Yiddish, he described the machine-gunning and shelling which heralded the Jordanian attack. The children took shelter and began reciting Psalms. "Then," with big eyes, "the soldiers came, and there was fighting, and the Arabs ran away." The child's interlocutor asks (unfairly perhaps), "So what won the war? The soldiers, or the psalms?"

"The psalms."

The psalms won the war. But there are (Jewish) soldiers, in a (Jewish) army, which, if defeated in war, leaves Jews (ultra-Orthodox, non-Orthodox, any Jew) in jeopardy of limb and life. The destiny of all is interlinked. The interdependence begins with life and death. And that

130

interdependence is even stronger when in the Land of Israel. It extends to politics, in the most telling sense and at the most direct experiential level. The Jewish Government can draft or defer, provide housing and education and financial grants and benefits. It issues identity cards and passports. It collects income taxes when it can, and indirect taxes which one can hardly evade.

Non-Orthodox men and women sometimes tour ultra-Orthodox neighborhoods, or visit family there. (And woe to the woman who dresses immodestly in some of the ultra neighborhoods.) Their bearing, their clothing, their inter-personal relations are not seen on the forbidden television screen or in the prohibited but widely read secular press. (Emulating the secular, and attempting to build more effective walls, one daily and at least three ultra-Orthodox weeklies appear in Israel, motivated in part by the desire and need to provide a "kosher" alternative to the blandishments, especially the provocative photographs appearing in the daily press. Nor is there coverage of the profane: sports, entertainment, the arts.)

All of these contacts bring the ultra from time-to-time cheek by jowl with the non-Orthodox. A vital economic dialectic is at work. In spite of government cushioning and "internal" financing from within the ultra communities, families need to have a livelihood. For example, the job market for graduates of the Beit Ya'acov women teachers' seminaries has shrunk. Consequently, women seeking a career have begun to expand their horizons beyond teaching. The Beit Ya'acov curriculum now offers courses in computing, graphics, professional sewing and bookkeeping. There is no question that these women will be forced to seek work outside the system and to train for jobs that demand higher and higher levels of knowledge and skills. Professor Menachem Friedman, an expert on the haredi communities, points out that haredi women will become increasingly better educated and feel more at home in the larger society while their husbands are left further and further behind, receiving little or no career preparation. This could have an explosive effect on haredi life. Perhaps it is not coincidental that although divorce is still relatively rare among the haredim, it is on the rise, and most of the divorces in the community are initiated by women. With greater awareness of women's rights and of outreach family guidance services, it seems that both in Israel and in the Diaspora there are more reported cases of wife-beating and child-abuse.

Haredi women leave the cocoon. They see another life, another life-style, another type of man-woman relations, another mode of dress, of "freedom" and openness. And, perhaps most devastating, *they see men who are usually the main (or at least equal) breadwinners.* It would only be natural for these women to ask themselves, and possibly their husbands, some penetrating questions. This issue becomes more acute as the world economic recession affects major ultra-Orthodox supporters of these institutions, and as Israeli government subsidies come under increasing scrutiny.

The success of haredism bears within itself the seeds of its own destruction. The infrastructure will not be able to grow indefinitely, to support a population which is constantly increasing. Haredi women raise large families, often becoming pregnant every year, with contraception forbidden. Those who are employed must go back to work within three months of having given birth since their family's livelihood depends on it.

For men, the employment possibilities in the haredi sector are indeed limited. There is a large gray economy operating in the ultra world. As long as younger men are registered in kollelim or yeshivot, they are exempt from the military. Service and sales businesses are often conducted from the home, and never appear in the books of the Income Tax Department, for, once registered with tax authorities, one is no longer a student, and is liable to be called to the colors.

Clearly haredi women and men are facing occupational dilemmas. Professor Friedman asks: "What happens when people can't make it? It will be a great tragedy when it becomes clearer that this isolation from, combined with dependence on modern society has come to a dead end."

Haredi society is far from monolithic: doubtless there will remain groups who continue defining themselves through their rejection of modernity in general, and Israeli society in particular. Yet is seems likely that because of economic pressures many eventually may have to turn toward fuller participation in the economic life of the country.

There can be no society numbering tens of thousands of students which does not contain many who are not cut out to be scholars. These young men are trapped. Their societal frame of reference, their families, their peers permit them neither to toil nor spin, neither to study a trade nor profession. They cannot drop out of yeshivah or kollel and join the army, or take a job. If they leave the cocoon, they are cut off from spiritual, material and personal support groups. Many of them suffer immense pain when confronted by the choice. A few make the break openly. The vast majority stay: overtly they are no different from anyone else in their area, but they only go through the motions.

Troubled or more enlightened parents, realizing their sons are not studying, and are unhappy, will permit their sons to find — or even will seek out for them — places of occupation or employment. The occupation could be as a volunteer in an Orthodox institution or hospital, which bears no compensation. Employment could be helping out in one of the gray ultra-Orthodox economy stores or services; or it could be a simple form of brokerage: financial deals, real estate, and so on. *Just don't record the occupation or employment: it might reach the attention of the authorities.* Don't even call volunteer work in a hospital "national service;" that smacks too much of Zionism, of collaborating with the state.

Other such conflicted young men become what is known with disdain as *shabaabnikim*: "low class."[1] They find ways to wheel and deal, dress to a T, within the socio-cultural frame of course, drive cars, own portable phones. The press reports visits to prostitutes by ultra-Orthodox men, and there are rumors of homosexual contacts in certain Jerusalem parks. These are surely a tiny minority, and may include non-dropouts. Though such incidents do occur, it would be unfair to tarnish the entirety of ultra-Orthodoxy with a broad brush.

Other dropouts find refuge in politics. They are the activists, the demonstrators, the stand-by squad. They are the ones who will reap rewards in terms of "jobs for the boys" and perks if their candidate, their bloc, their coterie makes it to power, just like the secular politicians. And in the ultra-ultra community, they may become the "enforcers:" members of a strike force called the Modesty Patrol.

The Modesty Patrol was first established in Jerusalem in 1920, and was then formed in Bnei Brak to battle the inroads of modernization. Married men conducting illicit affairs, or married women (usually those who have left the cocoon to work "out there") who breach the rules of modest behavior are followed, given stern warnings, and — if they persist — face "disciplinary action." The Patrol "casts its fear over the community," according to a press report, and well it may. It operates with the approval of certain rabbis and acts as enforcers for rabbinical courts in some cases. New problems involve porno video cassettes, and immodest wigs: a committee exists to censor wig fashions.*

Uglier aspects of modernization and secularization invade the ultra-Orthodox (and Orthodox) communities which have prided themselves as being drug-free and crime-free. The inroads of modern life, and the points of contact between the ultra-Orthodox and Orthodox communities and the non-Orthodox have changed the pristine image. For example, the press reported that an electronics teacher from an Orthodox village near Jerusalem, "and a Jerusalem yeshivah student were arrested. . . on suspicion of selling *more than half a kilo of cocaine* to undercover police officers."**

Another press report: *"Yeshivah students in Bnei Brak revealed to be drug addicts."*** The report, somewhat more restrained than the headline, speak of "forty-four drug addicts, some of whom are yeshivah students. . . in Bnei Brak. Most are regular users of cocaine, which they sniff, but they include users of hard drugs."

Some of the users were "truly ultra-Orthodox," others are Orthodox and traditional.

The phenomena described above are as pronounced — or even more pronounced in the Diaspora than in Israel. Below are some quotations about the situation in the ultra-Orthodox community in New York:****

> "They know that there are drugs here, that there is child abuse, compulsive gambling, AIDS. . . but hardly anyone talks about it." [The persons interviewed] believe that at least 15% of the city's 150,000 Hasidim also need help and are too terrified to seek it. "There is an enormous amount of prescription drug abuse, and outrageous sexual acting out with hookers, [as well as] gambling. Every sect — Satmer, Ger, Belz, Bobov — they all have a taste of it. They know it's there. . . ." The number of

---

* *Yediot Aharonot*, Tel Aviv, Weekly Magazine (*Shiv'ah Yamim*), June 9, 1989, pp. 23–27.

** *The Jerusalem Post*, March 30, 1989, p. 12. Emphasis added.

*** In *Yediot Aharonot*, Tel Aviv, by Devorah Namir, July 20, 1989, p. 9.

**** "Hooked Hasidim" in *New York* Magazine, January 28, 1991, pp. 31–36.

observant Jews participating in twelve-step recovery programs is rising daily, according to Jeff Neipris, Executive Director of the Jewish Alcoholics, Chemically Dependent Persons, and Significant Others Foundation, funded by UJA.

The Israeli press reports "a sex orgy" caught by the Modesty Patrol, its participants beaten mercilessly.* Those caught *in flagrante* were "from very good ultra homes." "Later," the reporter writes, " [the Patrol] gathered about one thousand shocked parents of the most extreme ultra-Orthodox groups in the Beit Ya'acov School." The report claimed that such happenings were not unknown in other areas of Jerusalem as well.

The uglier manifestations of modernity and secularism threaten the community. Even seemingly innocent pursuits are suspect: video-recording of wedding ceremonies have been prohibited by some ultra-Orthodox rabbis. Not, as one might hope, because the bright lights and antics of the photographer invade a sacred and private moment, but because of opposition to having TV and videos penetrate the home.**

The Patrol's use of force is not an innovation. It stems in part from the closed nature of the society, the hysteria and rumor-mongering which exist in such an inward-looking cauldron, and the lack of desire — actually, the inability — to turn to normal ("Zionist") peace-keeping forces. The tradition of force is not new; violence has never been un-known in Orthodoxy. Rabbinic authorities clash or are "offended" by a rival sect, and then inflamed followers may clash physically. Such "ideological" violence has a long history.

Today, followers of rival hasidic rabbis, supporters of differing rab-binical courts mount a psychological battle beginning with posters vilifying rivals and ending with blows, ambushes, and even desecration of tombs. The posters are verbal violence: screeds of hatred, poured out upon a rival group or a rival person, crammed with holy language and Biblical and rabbinic citations. They are posted on the walls and adver-tising hustings in ultra neighborhoods.

---

* *Kol Ha'Ir*, Jerusalem, "Ultra-Orthodox Orgy in Ramot," by Sara Ilan, March 3, 1989.

** "Rabbis: No to Record Weddings on Video," *Yediot Aharonot*, December 17, 1990, p. 16.

Beatings and fist-fights between contending sects reach new highs. A leading rabbi of one branch of the extreme anti-Zionist ultra-ultra-Orthodox, the *Netorei Karta* had acid thrown in his face, supposedly on the background of elections to the Meah She'arim residents' committee.* Violence may very well be enhanced by the example of State use of force in Israel, and the tradition of the pre-state underground movements.

ENGLISH-SPEAKING HAREDIM

There are influences on the haredi community which change its nature from within. One of them is the relatively large number of English-speaking haredim who either come to Israel from haredi families, or who enter its ranks as Ba'alei Teshuvah. English is heard in "the haredi street," as the press calls it. Many institutions, especially in Jerusalem cater to ultra- (and modern) Orthodox students from abroad. Some come to study and return, some to find a mate and stay. The institutions are never "mixed"— that is co-ed — and some of the women's institutions are of a remarkably high educational standard.

Some of the English-speaking haredim may also bring a broader approach, somewhat more openness towards Western society. Many have university degrees in many fields: from psychology to physics, and from computers to medicine. This element, halachically and socially in the same camp, is nonetheless different. They have seen another world, and in rejecting it, some of its dust, dross, and perhaps even positive values cling to them. They may also be more open to other aspects of Western culture, music, perhaps, or literature. The women are much "more liberated" in that they too, perhaps even more than the men, have learned a trade, or mastered a profession, or have academic training.

These differences show a face of haredism which is much more involved with the state. Men who have a profession must serve in the reserves; they are accustomed to voting in their countries of origin, of being active in politics, and certainly, on the municipal level have a tradition of involvement. They may also have less difficulty in relating to the non-Orthodox with whom they necessarily must work.

---

* According to a Kol Yisrael (Israel Radio) report, December 20, 1990. *Netorei Karta* = The Guardians of the City.

These influences of language, mentality, experience, and even dress, seem to spread over into two key areas of life: food habits and courting customs. The fast-food craze has invaded the haredi world. Young haredi Americans seem to be present in the many American-style fast food outlets in downtown Jerusalem. Their Israeli cousins or fellow-students may join them, and thus another area of contact, however distant, is opened.

The same type of more "open" haredi students, as well as strictly observant modern Orthodox young men and women may be seen courting in public. Couples may not be alone under any circumstances. Therefore earnest young people, at arm's length, touching being off-limits, may be found in conversation only in public places — hotel lobbies, street benches, and the most daring on well-lit and reasonably-frequented park paths, in "safe" places.

These young couples may have first been introduced through a professional matchmaker (*shadchan*), or, as often happens, by their teacher or head of yeshivah or girls' college, who feel the moral obligation to ensure a proper match. In the case of professional or family shadchan, chances are that the couple's background is too strict to permit them to meet even in public places without supervision. Those who do probably have been introduced by a fellow student, or parent of a student. To bring a young couple together is God's work.

Economic and cultural forces point to change, to a possible lowering of the walls. A key factor is the political involvement of the ultra-Orthodox parties. Ultra-Orthodox Cabinet Ministers have the right to vote on fateful cabinet decisions such as how to react to American pressure not to initiate a preventive strike against Iraqi missile and air bases during the Gulf War. Ultra-Orthodox Ministers not only had to take part in this decision, they also did not hesitate to explain to the media Israel's right to retaliate to attack. Making life-and-death decisions forces them to take prime responsibility for the system — within the system.

Similarly, when the cabinet faced a decision to permit foreign building laborers to enter Israel in their thousands to speed building for Russian immigrants, it was an ultra-Orthodox politician who led the battle on behalf of Israeli labor. That an Agudat Yisrael politician made common cause with the Histadrut Labor Federation reflected an historic shift of stance.

Prior to the expiration of the UN deadline on Iraq-Kuwait, both the [Zionist] Chief Rabbinate of Israel *and the ultra-Orthodox Council of Sages,* called for public prayers at the Western Wall. This was one of the few times Zionist and non-Zionist rabbinical sources cooperated. Politics makes strange bed-fellows, and the threat of war and gas attacks marvelously clears the mind.

The process of separation is intertwined with the process of secularization. As the threat from within mounts, one can expect extreme reactions from the ultra-Orthodox leadership. The breach is wide, and though some believe change is inevitable, the very fear of that change may make civil clashes more likely than civic peace. In that breach stands a small and even more beleaguered group, the modern (or centrist) Zionist Orthodox.

---

1. The word shabaabnikim shows an interesting cross-cultural confluence. *Shabaab* is the Arabic word for the street crowds, the "people," the unschooled and easily incited. The suffix "nik" is Russian, adapted into modern Hebrew by the early Russian pioneers, and tacked onto Hebrew words like kibbutz (Kibbutznik = a member of a kibbutz, etc.). The final suffix "-im" is the plural ending for masculine Hebrew words.

CHAPTER TWELVE

MODERN ORTHODOXY: ODD MAN OUT?

There is an odd man out in the construct of three evolving peoples. The modern Orthodox fall between two peoples. These "modern" or "centrist" or "Zionist" Orthodox do not fit into the ultra-Orthodox people. Nor are they part of the secular world.

Orthodox Jews believe Jewish law to be as binding as do the ultra-Orthodox. Both see the tradition as the framework for their lives: a direct line from the Torah at Sinai through the Oral Law to today's rabbinical authorities. But, although they may accept rulings from ultra-Orthodox rabbis, they seek their legitimate halachic authority from Zionist rabbis, and in Israel from the "official" Chief Rabbinate. These rabbis are more involved in the life and realities of Israel; in the Diaspora, they are certainly in tune with the day-to-day life of their congregants.

In the Diaspora, modern Orthodox rabbis are also graduates of colleges and universities; in Israel, though, the "Zionist" rabbis have not usually received a higher "secular" (academic) education. But they do, as a rule, embrace the state and serve in the military. The Orthodox live the civil religion and share the experiential realities of their non-Orthodox fellow-citizens.

The modern Orthodox also share much with the ultra-Orthodox. Thus, the rhythm of the Orthodox week is like the ultra-Orthodox one: beginning on Sunday, it works its way towards Friday evening, when the Sabbath begins, an "island in time," devoted to family life, prayer and study. On Saturday night after dark, the week begins again.

Like the ultra-Orthodox, although sometimes with less intensity or demonstrativeness, the Orthodox lifestyle revolves around the institutions of Jewish Law. Men may attend the synagogue daily where in addition to praying and studying, they see their neighbors and solidify the sense of community. Communal prayer is held again in the afternoon and evening. Some of course pray at home. Many Orthodox Jews will often devote a certain time of the day or week to studying Torah, or Talmud either in organized classes, with a friend or on their own.

Again, like the ultra-Orthodox, Orthodox parents generally prefer to send their children to separate schools: day schools in the Diaspora, "religious-state" schools in Israel. These Israeli schools combine religion and modernity. Not as limited as the ultra-Orthodox ones, they center upon the traditional Jewish curriculum, exploiting modern pedagogic techniques, together with the state program of general studies.

Israeli Orthodox teenagers are expected to be active in Zionist youth movements which have similarities to the secular youth movements or scouts. Upon graduation from high school the young men join the army either in the regular army three-year track or the more studious may opt for the combined yeshivah/army service program which takes five years. Thus they combine the traditional emphasis on Torah study with service to the state, and fulfill their civil requirements before joining the mainstream in their careers.

Orthodox girls are exempt from regular military service; many nonetheless volunteer for the full two-year stint, while the others perform volunteer full-time "national service" in hospitals and schools. Unlike the ultra-Orthodox, to these young people the state is not a hostile or at best neutral environment. The State of Israel is seen as part of the redemption of Israel and the world — a positive religious value.

It is therefore at this point — joining the mainstream — where the major differences with the ultra-Orthodox come to light. It is a demarcation line historically as well as in the present. After all, "Orthodoxy" in its separate organized form is a modern phenomenon: until modern times "all our great-great-grandparents were fully observant;" no special name was needed for those who kept the Halachah. Orthodoxy emerged as only one of several reactions to the challenges of the Enlightenment and the Emancipation. Organized Orthodox Judaism arose to preserve and protect traditional Jewish institutions, structures and values from the influences of secularization in the general culture, and from liberalizing tendencies within Judaism itself.

The Zionist movement was essentially a secular movement intent on radically changing the Jewish situation. To many Orthodox Jews it was perceived as one more manifestation of the penetration of modern ideas and values, another form of assimilation. The term ultra-Orthodox did not yet exist but the phenomenon was already alive: those who opposed the inroads of modern secular culture opposed Zionism with an equal militancy. This was the dividing line between what became known as ultra-Orthodoxy as distinguished from Orthodoxy. The main enemy of these "separatist" Orthodox Jews was secularization and assimilation; in their eyes, Zionism was the concrete embodiment of both.

There was though, early on in Zionism, a moderate Orthodox stream: the Mizrachi, whose slogan was, "The Land of Israel to the People of Israel according to the Torah of Israel." It saw Zionism as an ideal fully consonant with true Jewishness. The Mizrachi mission then was to lay the groundwork for a modern state, yet one guided by the laws of the Torah. The old-line "separatist" Orthodoxy opposed this openness bitterly. First of all, it meant cooperating with the secularists. Moreover, Zionism sought to end the state of exile. It was therefore clearly involving itself in a redemptive process: an attempt by *man* to redeem the people and Land of Israel. According to the old Orthodox view, redemption was to be initiated and carried out only by God, through the Messiah or a prophet.

This opposition was organized on two fronts: in Europe, and in Palestine, where the ultra-Orthodox "faithful" of the Old *Yishuv* felt particularly threatened by the influx of new Zionist settlers. In order to counter modernizing influences, and to combat Zionist activity, and particularly the Mizrachi Orthodox, anti-modernists and anti-Zionists in Europe organized an umbrella organization in 1912 called Agudat Yisrael. The anti-Zionist position was expressed in the manifesto of the organization:

> The Jewish people stands outside the framework of the political peoples of the world and differs essentially from them. The Sovereign of the Jewish people is the Almighty; the Torah is the Law that governs them, and the Holyland has been at all times destined for the Jewish people. It is the Torah which determines all actions for Agudat Yisrael.

The Mizrachi position was clearly Zionist: all Jews who participate in redeeming the Land of Israel and in the ingathering of the exiles of the Jewish people, whether religious or not, are agents in God's scheme of redemption. The leading spokesman for this religious approach to modern Zionism was Rabbi A.Y. Kook, Chief Ashkenazi Rabbi from 1921 to 1935, when he died. Rabbi Kook saw modern Zionism as part of the messianic process, *At-halta de-geula*, the Beginning of the Redemption. In his view, fulfillment of the commandments to settle the Land of Israel and to make it fruitful overrode hesitations regarding cooperation with secular Jews; on the contrary, this was a positive virtue, a mitzvah.* He taught a heady mix of religious mysticism based on love of people and land which embraced all Jews, both secular and religious. His students were inculcated with the redemptive quality of religious Zionism. His spirituality, literary talent and openness made him persona grata even among the virulently anti-religious secularists, especially in the labor movement.

Modern Orthodox Jews tend to live by the dictum, *"Torah im Derech Eretz,"* combining the traditional, *Orthodox* lifestyle with "the way of the world." This combination of Orthodox behavior and openness to the world was presented by an American theological figure along these lines: since Judaism is truth, it can withstand the clash with other ideas. The ideal Jew is the one who succeeds in maintaining a religous lifestyle and educating his or her children while contributing to the larger society and enjoying much of what it has to offer. This is the approach of the late Rabbi Joseph Dov (Ber) Soleveitchik (1903-1993) of Boston, the dominant figure at Yeshiva University, mentor of generations of modern Orthodox rabbis and lay people in North America.** He also taught that Jews regardless of differences in theology and practice should cooperate on matters affecting general Jewish interests and Israel.

---

* Zvi Yaron, *Mishnato Shel HaRav Kook* [The Teachings of Rabbi Kook], Jerusalem, WZO, 1974. A more recent study is Benjamin Ish-Shalom, *Harav Kook, Bein Ratzionalism le-Mystica* [Rabbi Abraham Isaac Kook — Between Rationalism and Mysticism], Tel Aviv, 'Am 'Oved, 1990.

** Soloveitchik, a great Talmudist and Judaic scholar, descended from outstanding Talmudists of Volozhin and Brisk (Brest-Litovsk). He also won a Ph.D. from the University of Berlin in philosophy, which in itself marks him from most ultra-Orthodox religious leaders. Rabbi Soloveitchik, known to Western Orthodoxy simply as "the Rav" — *the* Rabbi — was an avowed religious Zionist.

Today, modern Orthodoxy in Israel and the Diaspora is unequivo-
cally Zionist, mainly an heir of the Mizrachi ideology. Diaspora modern
Orthodoxy is more and more influenced by Israel. The tendencies of late
for Zionist Orthodoxy to become less open and more rightist in
nationalist terms spreads strongly into the Diaspora.

The change flowed to some extent from the teachings of the son of
Chief Rabbi Kook, Rabbi Tzvi Yehuda Kook. Himself a gentle man, his
disciples translated his fervor linking redemption of the people to the
holiness of the Land of Israel into a rather aggressive nationalism. The
Gush Emunim (The Block of the Faithful) movement to settle Judea and
Samaria (the West Bank) and Gaza sprang from his yeshivah. Israeli
politics and religion have been irreversibly changed by the school of
thought it represents. It has combined extra-parliamentary action with
political activism.

The range of modern Orthodoxy in Israel is thus halachic, with
varying stresses on nationalism, ranging from a socialistic tendency and
moderate nationalism, as symbolized by the Orthodox Kibbutz Movement (*Ha-Kibbutz Ha-Dati*) through to the Gush Emunim, and to even
more extreme Orthodox ultra-nationalists. The extremes have become
stronger; the moderates more pressed. The seeds of chauvinist religious
nationalism coexist here with a basic commitment to democracy. There
is a battle within the souls of these "National" or Zionist Orthodox between the two principles: democracy, and Divine Will.

The Zionist Orthodox as part of the state system see elections, the
ballot box and legislation as an instrument to advance their ideology. On
occasion, therefore they may make common cause and a united front
with the ultra-Orthodox. But the modern Orthodox do not see the state
system simply as one to be exploited. If the ultra-Orthodox prefer to
await the Messiah in their communities, the modern Orthodox hope is
diametrically the opposite: to participate in the process and spur his
coming. Thus their practice of the civil religion of the State is infused
not only with patriotism but with religious fervor. The Mizrachi tradition
reflects itself in military service, in the large numbers of Orthodox students in Israeli universities, and the existence of a Mizrachi-sponsored
university, Bar-Ilan, and of an Orthodox technical institute, the
Jerusalem Institute of Technology.

This participation in the life of the nation together with the non-Orthodox secular majority is the hallmark of today's modern Orthodox National Religious Party, known also by its Hebrew acronym, *Mafdal*. The NRP has participated in almost every coalition since 1948. Its representation though has been weakened partly because Sephardi traditionalists who used to vote for it have shifted their support to Sephardi parties such as Shas, and partly because more extreme nationalist parties have drawn away voters. The result is that Mafdal goes along with a me-too nationalist line whether because many of its members believe in it and out of fear of losing the little it still has.

Another modern Orthodox party, *Meimad*, a more gentle version of the original Mafdal ran in the 1988 Knesset elections on a platform of distancing the state from religious legislation, and a dovish view on the Palestinian issue. Since Meimad did not even receive enough votes to elect one member to the Knesset, its influence must be seen as small, despite the popularity of its leaders among elements of the Orthodox population. It may yet reappear on the political scene, thus further weakening Mafdal.

By staying within the system and almost always holding cabinet posts, Mafdal retains patronage strength for its hard core. By way of contrast, Agudat Yisrael began to play a more active role in coalitions in 1977. NRP members have assumed important portfolios, such as Education, Interior, or the Ministry for Religious Affairs. The NRP has used these positions to build the state-controlled religious school system and other institutions, such as the Chief Rabbinate.

ORTHODOX — ULTRA-ORTHODOX: HOW CLOSE? HOW FAR?

Fundamental differences exist between the ultra-Orthodox and the Zionist Orthodox. However, there are ways in which ultra-Orthodoxy influences the more moderate. For instance, many Orthodox Jews today are assuming some of the modest dress requirements in the style of the haredim. Although the men will not wear the ultra uniforms of long *peyot*, long coats and special hats, today one does see many more Orthodox married women covering their heads than just a few years ago. This strictness may be a result of yeshivah and Orthodox women's equivalent education, often with teachers out of the ultra camp. Possibly as well, the Orthodox community fears that it looks less "legitimately Torah-true" than the ultra-Orthodox. Generally speaking, the military command, "To the right — dress," applies to the ultra and Orthodox camps; they line up on the right marker. The center in "centrist Orthodoxy" has shifted rightwards.

The line blurs in personal commitment to Halachah. Both groups see the Halachah as a direct line from Sinai, both live their lives according to the rhythm of the Jewish calendar and both give their existence meaning with the belief in a personal God. Religiously they remain one people because they recognize each other's Jewishness in basic ways: conversion, marriage, divorce and the like. It is not impossible for ultra-Orthodox Jews to be found in Orthodox synagogues on weekday or Sabbath mornings, or vice versa. They may have differences in the way they dress or how they observe the dietary laws — or at most differences over which rabbinic authority certifies kashrut — but they both observe them. They may have different role models and leaders they respect. Yet they study the same Talmud, read the same commentators and the Orthodox accept most of the same past rabbinic authorities as the ultras. Though the modern Orthodox also watch television, attend concerts and go to movies, they still have, in the halachic sense, a common language of discourse with the ultra-Orthodox. That language no longer binds either group with the great number of secular Israelis or non-Orthodox Jews elsewhere.

If the day were to come when the religious schism in the Jewish people actually occurred, and modern Orthodox Jews had to decide where they stood, would they therefore place themselves firmly in the "Torah Camp"? After all, in spite of the shared language, they are not fully at home with their haredi brethren: there is one basic halachic difference. The ultra-Orthodox will have nothing to do with the "official" rabbinate: they do not recognize the halachic decisions and status of the Chief Rabbinate, which they see as a Zionist creation. Mizrachi wanted to create a "national" rabbinate, that is a central authority, a Chief Rabbinate selected at the time under a statutory procedure of the pre-state Council of the Yishuv, the *Va'ad Leumi*. With statehood, the Chief Rabbinate acts under Israeli statute law. Its roots can be traced to the role of the *Haham Bashi*, the Chief Rabbi of the Jews in Palestine under the Ottoman Empire. A British Mandatory Ordinance of 1920 recognized two Chief Rabbis — Ashkenazi and Sephardi, the latter known as the *Rishon Letzion*, the First in Zion. In 1980 the Knesset passed the Law of the Chief Rabbinate of Israel, which sits atop a hierarchy of religious councils and institutions in communities around the country.[1]

The Chief Rabbinate, though, must be a disappointment to the early Mizrachi thinkers, who were sure that such a central authority would react to Jewish independence by updating Halachah, and adapting it to national independence. But the Chief Rabbinate suffers from an innate inferiority complex vis-a-vis the ultra Rabbinate, and from a lack of civic courage. The rabbis elected lean more and more rightward.

Since the Zionist Orthodox see the state as an expression of Divine Will, their patriotism is unquestioned, and respected by most non-observant Israelis. Some, though, see zealous nationalistic Orthodox Zionism as a Messianic aberration: a combination of strict modern Orthodox piety and nationalist chauvinism. They view this Messianism as the marriage of the second Rav Kook's mystic approach to the holiness of the Land of Israel merged with irredentist tendencies.

This intoxicating mixture can be traced through *Gush Emunim* (The Block of the Faithful) who were responsible for much of the settlement in Judea, Samaria and Gaza, to the extreme groups which found Begin's Likud too tame, and formed more extreme parties. Most Orthodox Jews in the Diaspora lean towards the hard-liners on political issues, though not necessarily to the extreme.[2]

The ugliest marriage of Zionist Orthodoxy and nationalist chauvinism is *Kach,* the group founded by the late Meir Kahane, which is both anti-Arab and anti-democratic. It is not only a perversion of religion but a perversion of the teachings of the father of Revisionism, Zeev (Vladimir) Jabotinsky who espoused a liberal-democratic yet hardline nationalism. Chauvinism is not the sole purview of Kach.

The mix of ultra-Orthodoxy and ultra-nationalism creates odd ideological types which do not classify easily. In an interview with an ultra-Orthodox yet ultra-nationalist rabbi, Yitzhak Ginsberg, the underlying clash of values is clearly seen:*

> If the law of the State is not Hebrew Law, then it is clearly not
> a state of Jews. If the State of Israel proclaims that all are
> equal, and that there are equal rights for all religions, this con-

---

* "The Rise of the Ginsberg Hassidim," *HaAretz* Magazine, Tel Aviv, by Yair Sheleg, July 14, 1989, p. 12 ff.; interview with Ginsberg, p. 13.

fusion works against us, against true Zionism. At some stage we shall have to face this basic question, we shall no longer be able to evade it: which document do we choose, the Torah of Moses or the Declaration of Independence.

This looks like a new brand of fundamentalism, a kind of anti-democratic or totalitarian Orthodoxy — or rather Halachacracy. It is a blend of extreme ultra-Orthodoxy cloaked in Mizrachi terminology, and intractable nationalism. That this is a hybrid shows only that many different kinds of fruits grow on the stem of Israeli Orthodoxy today.

In spite of these trends, the distinction between modern and ultra-Orthodoxy becomes clear once personal experience is considered: secular education, youth movements, interest in sports, music and other arts, academic studies, and above all military service and observing the civil religion. These shared experiential realities have their influence. In contrast to Rabbi Ginsberg, a member of an Orthodox kibbutz — still true to the old openness of Mizrachi — has another perspective:

> If people [i.e. Orthodox and non-Orthodox] do not discuss things together, they won't be able to serve in the army together, they won't be able to sit in the same tank together. In actuality, the state will not exist without this dialogue.*

Another young Orthodox kibbutznik:

> If one day we should read in the press that the Conservative and Reform movements voluntarily disbanded and closed all their synagogues and all their institutions — would that [day] be a holiday for Judaism? The Conservatives and Reform see themselves as a religious community.

Civil religion and shared experiences with the non-Orthodox form one watershed dividing the ultra-Orthodox from the Zionist Orthodox. Another watershed is loyalty to parliamentary democracy. There is a solid body among the Zionist Orthodox and their sympathizers and sup-

---

* *'Amudim* [The publication of Ha-kibbutz Ha-dati; The Religious Kibbutz Movement], Vol. 37, 5 (Adar Alef, 5749 [February, 1989]) "We Shall March Together — Realization of a Slogan," p. 153 ff.

porters who are part-and-parcel of the parliamentary democratic process: there is even a small coterie of peace activists. When the chips are down, on a clear democracy/anti-democracy issue, many of the moderate Orthodox would throw in their lot with the non-Orthodox, or so one feels today. In fact, the modern Orthodox are seen as closer to the secular by the ultras themselves, as is illustrated by the following anecdote recounted by Professor Avi Ravitzky at a public lecture at the Hebrew University. At an ultra-Orthodox wedding he attended, not only were men and women separated into different rooms, but the ultra-Orthodox men were also seated in a room by themselves, and the modern Orthodox and non-Orthodox were seated in another room — together.*

The modern Orthodox are caught on the horns of a dilemma, and as all Israel has become more extreme in politics *and* religion since 1967, it is harder and harder to predict behavior. External affairs: defense and relations with the Arabs within the pre-1967 borders, as well as with the Arab states will occupy a place of primacy in national concern and national politics. The *kulturkampf*, the struggle over Israel's eventual civil image and life may be postponed. Nonetheless, legislation concerning abortion, pork and Sabbath observance are already seen by secularists as a further escalation of that kulturkampf.

Should Arab-Israeli external relations, or the Judea-Samaria situation change, that is, should the Arab problem stop being the major divide in Israeli life today, the hardening of lines between the ultra-Orthodox and the other Israelis would become more pronounced. We then might find the moderate Orthodox tending towards the majority, and distancing themselves from the ultras.

If the question of Halachah becomes bound up with the question of returning areas of Judea and Samaria — that is if the interests of ultra-Orthodoxy merge with those of the (armed and trained) ultra-nationalists, the choices will be more severe.

In brief, the Zionist Orthodox should be seen basically as part of the "secular" or non-Orthodox consensus on all issues except blatantly halachic ones. This definition will make modern Orthodox Jews uncomfortable. It is nonetheless valid should democracy as a way of life be put to the test. But that validity is shifting. . . .

---

* The lecture took place on December 31, 1990.

A word about that ugliest of all terms: civil war. Almost no modern state has been spared a civil war of one kind or another. Often these have been over basic rights and constitutional issues. The boundaries of consensus, history teaches, are shaped by conflict. The conflict to establish a consensus for co-existence between those who place Halachah over the State and those who would fight for parliamentary (yes, in essence, secular) democracy has led to limited physical violence in the past. An Israel at relative peace with the Palestinians and Arabs will not be at peace internally over the religious issue. The tragic conflict-to-come seems inevitable. Israeli Jews are so busy with the Arab issue that they are not dealing with the Jewish one. It will not be postponed forever.

---

1. The role of the Chief Rabbinate as an instrument of state has been criticized not only by ultras, but by the iconoclastic yet quite Orthodox Professor Yeshayahu Leibowitz. He believes that Ben Gurion continued the institution of the Chief Rabbinate in order to tame it, so to speak, to harness and subjugate Orthodoxy to the state. Some of Leibowitz's most scathing attacks are also reserved for the teachings of Rav Kook, whose mysticism and nationalism he sees as a perversion which has raised love for the Land into a form of idolatry.

2. The stress on national symbols in religious terms brings to mind the new role of the *Kotel*, the last remnant of the Second Temple Wall. The reverence and beauty, even solace and sense of union with the past and holy, has been thoroughly elevated in folk religion and especially by extreme nationalists, whether Orthodox or not, to a new idolatry: Kotelatry.

CHAPTER THIRTEEN

ORTHODOX-SECULAR RELATIONS

"I didn't agree with Golda Meir, but I could talk to her," [an ultra-Orthodox] spokesman said. "With the present secular leaders who were already the third generation to leave religion, there was no longer a common language. . . ."

From *The Jerusalem Post*, July 7, 1991

A street scene in Jerusalem. On one of the main streets in the center of the city, King George Avenue, cars stop at a traffic light. It is just the hour that children are off to school, and the pedestrian crossing is full of children. A group of ultra-Orthodox girls, perhaps 12- or 13-year-olds, crosses. They are distinguishable by their long sleeved-dresses, in somber tones, and long hemlines. One young woman driver, modern and attractive, rolls down her window and shouts: "You forgot your pantyhose!" The reference is to the required modesty in dress these children observe. But the tone is one of . . . hatred? . . . disgust? . . . certainly anger. The dispassionate observer cannot but be shocked by the depth of passion, vented upon a group of innocent schoolgirls. . . .

An ultra-Orthodox young man approaches a group of young Israelis and suggests they put on the phylacteries (tefillin) he proffers. A non-Orthodox youngster growls: "When you go to the army like us, I'll talk to you. . . ."

An ultra-Orthodox young man is collecting for a charity. One householder opens the door and says, "If it's for your draft-dodgers forget it."

A demonstration at the Knesset. . . . Kibbutz members who are engaged in pig-raising are joined by civil libertarians protesting the new law to prohibit sale of pork products and pig-farming. One of their placards shows a picture of a pig-like face, with a black Orthodox hat and beard, captioned, "Today — pig! Tomorrow — you!" An ultra-

Orthodox Knesset member walked away in disgust. "It reminds me of the anti-Semitic placards in Poland before World War II." And indeed it does. . . . Worse, a pig's head was placed in a synagogue in Bnei Brak, inscribed "I'm haredi too!"

The surging power of ultra-Orthodoxy and the control its parties exercise over the fate of coalitions are creating a strong and potentially vicious backlash among Israel's secular. And since the secular are plugged into the liberal Jewish elements in the United States and other Diaspora countries, the anger boils over into the Diaspora. In reaction to a series of "religious" laws passed by the Knesset, Tel Aviv's then Mayor, Shlomo Lahat said: "It is regrettable that the radical religious groups . . . bring up such laws, which *only arouse the general public's hatred of religious people.*"*

In trying to breach the cooperation between Orthodox and ultra-Orthodox in one series of coalition negotiations, Yossi Beilin, a spokesman for the Labor Party, said to a group of Mafdal (Zionist-Orthodox) oriented politicians:**

> The truth is that only with you do we have a shared language. We live together, go to the army together, study and teach in the universities together. Among all the Orthodox, only you identify with the state, with the Zionist enterprise. We and you have rights and responsibilities.
>
> What do we have in common with "them" [the ultra-Orthodox], who have only rights but no responsibilities, not even for military service? Their world is so narrow — they do not even know a bit of history or English. . . . Their children study in Yiddish, and when they grow up they dodge military service. . . . They are so different from us, while you are so similar to us.

The anger will also probably turn upon the moderate Orthodox. The

---

* *The Jerusalem Post,* December 18, 1990, Front Page, "Tel Aviv to Party on Shabbat."

** *Ma'ariv: (Shabbat Section)* (Tel Aviv), "Does Peres Have a Narrow Government?" Section B, p. 1, March 9, 1990.

radicalization of the ultra-Orthodox parties has had the effect of pushing the formerly moderate NRP (*Mafdal*) further to the right religiously. Partly this is due to the demographic change in Israel, with populistic leadership ascendant in Mafdal, and partly due to a need to be seen as being *plus catholique que le Pape.*

The Orthodox have tinted the State with a patina of piety and a coloration of official religious ceremony. From the very start of renewed Jewish sovereignty, the Orthodox have opposed the adopting of a constitution, since this would displace "our constitution which is the Torah."

They did manage to ensure fulfillment of every section of the pre-State four-part "Status Quo Agreement of 1947." That agreement between Ben Gurion and the Agudat Yisrael guaranteed: 1) rabbinic jurisdiction over personal status (marriage, divorce and conversion); 2) religious education networks: today, the State religious system and the "independent" ultra-Orthodox systems; 3) the maintenance of Kashrut in all public institutions; 4) the observance of Shabbat in public places and government (including military) facilities.

Having achieved so much of their agenda on the eve of Israeli Independence, the Orthodox have since stepped up pressure to further increase their influence. Many of these victories are attributable to the negotiating skills of Mafdal, the National Religious Party. In the pre-State era, and continuing until 1977, the Mafdal had closely cooperated with the Labor Party on economic, security and foreign policy. They were in part "rewarded" with the gains listed above. The knowledge that less compromising parties, especially Agudat Israel were pressing in the wings often helped Mafdal. On occasion, the Orthodox and ultra-Orthodox parties made common front to forward their agenda.

When the Likud came to power in 1977, the influence of ultra-Orthodoxy grew, reenforced by Agudah and newer competing ultra-Orthodox parties, especially those supported by a newly-conscious Sephardi electorate. The latter had become the swing vote and could determine which of the two contending camps would form the government, the right-leaning Likud, or the left-leaning Labor and allied parties.

ULTRA-ORTHODOX POLITICAL PARTIES

Given the special religious and ideological nature of this constituency, it is no wonder that more than one party fights for its votes. Agudat

Yisrael, an Ashkenazi ultra-Orthodox party, was originally founded in Eastern Europe about 80 years ago, to combat Reform and Zionism. After the Holocaust, it chose a form of coexistence with Zionism, and held a monopoly on the ultra ground for decades. In rather simplistic terms, it was a combination of two major elements or traditions in Eastern European Jewry: the hasidic school which organized in camps of various charismatic "rebbes" tracing themselves back in linear ascent to the first followers of the Baal Shem Tov [c. 1700-1760]; and the "Lithuanians" who held studying Talmud and Talmudic commentators more important than following the path of the pietistic and joyful hasidic "rebbes."*

The Agudah in recent years faced a rebellion from the Sephardi younger elements whom they had influenced and controlled, through yeshivot, grants and other material benefits. Under this influence, they radicalized and transformed ("Ashkenized") their Sephardi brethren, who adopted their more rigid stance on religious observance in place of the gentler Sephardi tradition. To this day in the yeshivah world, the "best" students are sent to Ashkenazi schools, and usually only graduates of such yeshivot are considered knowledgeable enough to be Sephardi religious leaders.

However, once the flag of resentment was raised,the rebels flocked to the camp of a former Sephardi Chief Rabbi, himself a great scholar and decisor, Ovadiah Yosef, and formed a party called *Shas*. In basic terms, the rebellion was over Sephardi public status and self-pride, and of course over control of the "pie," State-administered and budgeted funds.

Issues of "ethnic" pride were perhaps more symbolic but no less important in the minds of some of the Sephardi public. These included the fact that Agudah meetings were held in Yiddish, and that Rabbi Ovadiah Yosef repeatedly had to defer to his Ashkenazi colleagues. Rabbi Schach, the leader of the anti-hasidic or Lithuanian group within Agudah, unhappy with the mounting hasidic power, encouraged the

---

* True, there was an important third element: the strict Halachic but nonetheless Westernized (often university-educated) German Jewish ultras. The influence of this stream has waned and all but disappeared; thus the emphasis on the two European streams.

birth of Shas, which did well in the 1988 elections. This significantly weakened Agudah political clout. (Shas's coalition with Labor and the left alliance Meretz in 1992 has driven Schach to turn against Shas.)

The besieged Agudah suffered another blow from the redoubtable Rabbi Schach who was still determined to weaken the hasidic grasp on the party. He encouraged yeshivah elements trained in the Lithuanian mode to found yet another ultra party, *Degel Hatorah* [The Flag of the Torah]. Tempers run high and the results, seen on election day in greater focus, are felt in sundered families and congregational and yeshivah tensions.

An example of how these political rifts shake the ultra community came across Israeli breakfast tables the morning of the 1989 municipal elections in Israel.*

Did he say 'Habad Hasidim aren't Jewish?' Rabbi Schach reportedly had said this regarding the followers of the Rebbe of Lubavitch. The reporter referred to "warfare that held sway between ultra-Orthodox parties during the national election" campaign. Another headline referring to an ultra stronghold: *"Fistfights, heated arguments and heckling at Bnei Brak rally."* A third report seems inconceivable: "Fistfights and *two attempts to run over rivals* marked last night's heated Agudat Yisrael rally..."

To compound all this even more, the Habad followers of Rabbi Schneerson of Lubavitch (now Brooklyn), who had kept themselves above the political fray, had thrown their support behind the Agudah in 1988 in order to force a change in the "Who is A Jew" legislation to the detriment of Conservative and Reform converts to Judaism. The attempt failed because Yitzchak Shamir chose to broke the agreements previously signed with the ultra-Orthodox by Likud. In 1992, Habad was less evident in haredi politics.

Though Byzantium is some hundreds of miles north of Jerusalem and a millennium-and-a-half distant, the politics of Israel are Byzantine with a vengeance. Even such seasoned political veterans as Labor leader Shimon Peres failed to understand, for example, that Degel Hatorah's dovish views on the Palestinian question did not mean support for a Labor government, since they are outweighed by Rabbi Schach's visceral hatred of the secular ideology of the Labor movement. Conversely,

---

* *The Jerusalem Post*, February 28, 1989. Emphasis added.

the more hawkish stance of the Agudah (under the influence of Rabbi Schneerson), did not mean it would support a Shamir government, since the hasidic courts were still seething over Shamir's broken promises regarding "Who is a Jew". Too many observers and politicians make the mistake of thinking that the issues they consider primary are necessarily those most important to the ultra-Orthodox world. The haredi parties exist first and foremost to ensure their own group's privileges. Every other issue is peripheral.

Given this balance-wheel power, some rabbis were able to place obstacles in the path of speedy and full acceptance of the Ethiopian Jews; they were able to postpone the extradition to France of a criminal, William Nakash, who had the benefit of two qualities: he was both Sephardi and a ba'al teshuvah. By virtue of their authority to supervise kashrut, pressure was stepped up on hotels and restaurants to prevent parties in celebration of the civil New Year. Most criticized by liberals has been their role in the defeat of the Human Rights Law. But a balance reasserts itself somewhat. Orthodoxy's demand to broaden the jurisdictional scope of rabbinical courts in matters of personal status has so far been withstood by an *ad hoc* coalition of secularists of all parties in the non-Orthodox spectrum.

A decade and more harvest of the Orthodox partnership in Likud or "National Unity" coalition governments shows eight or nine victories. Admittedly, some of these are of limited application but others have a significant impact on Israeli society. One of the most notable of these is in the field of education. Whereas the "independent" educational network of Agudat Israel (Ashkenazi) had operated even in pre-state days, there is now an additional ultra-Orthodox educational stream — the Sephardi Shas school system which has been the biggest new winner of state funds. Daily, well over 10,000 pupils attend one of the hundreds of newly established *El Hama'ayan* educational institutions run by Shas. They provide kindergarten, elementary school and supplementary after-school classes.

These new non-haredi supporters had in the past regarded haredim as being outside the pale, particularly because of their anti-national stance. But the "new men" of Shas gave voice to a traditional-nationalist fervor that swept up many erstwhile secular people, most of whom had been Likud supporters since 1977.

BACKLASH

In Jerusalem, tensions between Orthodox and non-Orthodox reached such a pass that one party ran in the municipal elections on a strikingly one-issue anti-Orthodox platform. In February 1989, they distributed a flyer showing "The Spread of the Ultra-Orthodox" in bold graphics on a map of Jerusalem neighborhoods, playing on secularist fears. Indeed, Jerusalem is increasingly a haredi city. However, in any other country, a similar map which showed "The Spread of Jews" would be condemned as anti-Semitic. Secular Israelis, even fairly laid-back types have for the most part become increasingly militant in their hostility to the ultra-Orthodox in the last few years. A possible explanation for such behavior, bordering on aggravated xenophobia, is their perception that the ultra-Orthodox are "winning". At the same time, some interpret the stepped-up assertiveness of the ultra-Orthodox to be caused by a sense of winning accompanied, paradoxically, by fears of losing.

Either way, the non-Orthodox backlash is mounting. The anger seethes. The disgusting spectacle of coalitionary haggling while Israel burns has turned more and more of the "ordinary folk" whether left- or right-leaning into anti-ultra voters.

"*I am sick and tired,*" the non-Orthodox man said, "*of the prostitutes of the haredi parties.*" "But why? They are only playing the game by the rules the non-Orthodox politicians made. If you call the ultras names, call the two main blocs panderers." The backlash spreads. For example, the hundreds of thousands of "Russian" immigrants know little of the ultras, and owe them nothing but anger because of their labelling a large number of immigrants as non-Jews.

TENSIONS: Zionism and Torah

Perhaps the greatest obstacle to rapprochement between the ultra-Orthodox and the rest of Israeli society is the question of army service for yeshivah students. The subject is epitomized in this citation:*

Last week, David Delarosa died in the aftermath of injuries he sustained while trying to rescue a mother and her children

---

* Gabi Bashan, "Genuine partnership," *HaAretz*, January 2, 1989.

caught on a burning bus. The bus had been set ablaze by fire bombs hurled at it in Jericho. As Delarosa ran toward the bus the father, "an outstanding yeshivah student," as he was later called, stood praying to God. . . .

The cardinal issue [in the to draft or not to draft yeshiva student question] is not about mutual acquaintance; how the secular and ultra-Orthodox can get to know each other. No! It is over mutual responsibility. Beyond extorting money from the State, what is the extent of the partnership as far as the ultra-Orthodox public is concerned?

But to focus on military service or its evasion is to see only the tip of an ideological glacier. Much more salient is the underlying motivation of both groups. Nathan Birnbaum [1864-1937] who coined the word "Zionism," subsequently went on to turn ultra-Orthodox and vehemently anti-Zionist. He then wrote: "I do not doubt that those who intend to make the Jews the same as the nations of the world are idolaters."*

Below is the transcript of a lecture by a rabbi to a selected group of students. Its title "Why We Should Mourn on Independence Day" betrays the true face of many yeshivot.

Let it be understood that I do not negate the achievement or character or path of Zionism, I come to negate its very essence. As a faithful religious Jew, I am more anti-Zionist than I am anti-Christian. . . . Christians and Muslims have attempted to destroy Jews physically. But they have never been able to destroy the soul of the Jew simply because they cannot reach it. Goyim cannot hurt us in terms of values, because their plane is the physical, and they cannot reach the plane of the Jews. . . .

Zionism, on the other hand, made history by separating Judaism from the Jew and sought to kill the first while saving the second. This is indeed its historical accomplishment. The goy never meant to hurt Judaism but just Jews. Zionism didn't

---

* In *'Am Ha-shem* [The People of God], Bnei Brak, Nezah Press, 1977.

intend to hurt Jews but to hurt Judaism. . . In the Holocaust six million Jews were destroyed. Zionism had destroyed tens of thousands by making them goyim. They do this without harming physically, so that Jews do not notice that they are being hurt. Christians didn't try to destroy Judaism but to say it was wrong. Zionists tried to destroy the idea of Judaism by saying it is something else. The Zionists say that I don't want Judaism but want to remain a Jew — this is its innovation.

As Rabbi Sa'adia Gaon stated, a Jew is a Jew because of his Torah. The reason the Jews are a nation is because one will creates a unity, the divine will. . . . And without the religious idea, there is no significance to the Jewish people. This is Judaism. One must accept it or not, but this is it. Every goy knows this. Zionism has reversed the whole thing, making the people the essence, Torah and culture secondary.

Yitzhak Breuer said, "Zionism has created collective assimilation." It is impossible to compare the Jewish people with other nations of the world, and this is just what Zionism has done. In seeking to be like unto all the nations, you stop being a Jew because you have lost the idea and the value.*

The rifts between believers and non-believers has its historic roots in this ideology versus the Zionist thrust for "normalcy." The rift between Israel of today and the Diaspora is also no historical accident. In flashback, the next chapter examines some of the beginnings of the schism cutting this people into three.

---

* Quoted by Janet Aviad, *Return to Judaism*, Chicago, University of Chicago Press, 1983.

CHAPTER FOURTEEN

FLASHBACK: EAST AND WEST IN JEWISH LIFE

THE EMANCIPATION AND THE JEWS OF EUROPE

Modern Jewish life is a reaction to the blinding potentiality of liberty, known as the Emancipation, which was presented to the Jews of Europe beginning roughly 200 years ago. Zionism and assimilation, ultra-Orthodoxy and Reform, Jewish Socialism and Cultural Autonomism all came about as a reaction to the opening of the gates of society.

Toward the end of the 18th century, civil rights began to be extended to the Jews of Europe. For a period of over a hundred years, progress was uneven. The Emancipation began in France, was carried on the wave of Napoleonic conquest, and leapfrogged from country to country, principality to principality. Seldom was it granted easily. As rights and privileges found acceptance in the statute books, racial anti-Semitism was born. This new form of Jew hatred built on deep-rooted xenophobia, on the old Church-inspired theological anti-Semitism and "scientific" racism.

The Emancipation grew out of another French contribution to mankind, the Enlightenment. It taught that humanity need not be encumbered by traditional answers and transmitted values. The "enlightened" held that free inquiry, liberty of intellect and the veracities of science outweighed theology, "revealed truth" and the divine order which had characterized the medieval period.

The initial impact on Jewish communities occasioned a twofold response. Jews could embrace enlightenment and emancipation, and cast off the yoke of tradition. In so doing, they would break through the barriers of civic disability and persecution to enter "the free new world." The other choice would be to entrench the rabbis and followers more deeply into the old ways. In other words, they could either embrace the new or withdraw into the shell of the old.

The non-Jewish political leaders who granted civil rights fostered a thrust towards assimilation. "The Jews should be denied everything as a nation, but granted everything as individuals," a parliamentarian said after the French Revolution.*

Jews in Western and Central Europe began to share the aspirations and the interests of the general, non-Jewish European population. By freeing themselves from the limitations of a separate Jewish existence, these Jews sought to enter European culture and society. In the beginning they changed their dress and language and adapted patterns of education and entertainment to those of the Europeans. These seemingly external signs of acculturation signalled changes of much deeper significance. First there was the change in the authority which legitimated and controlled norms and expectations. Secularizing Jews shunted aside much of the influence of the rabbis to make room for secular sources of authority: the law of the State or ethical codes believed to be the product of human reason. In Jewish life as in Christian society, the claims of a transcendent authority, or of the representatives of a tradition based on supernatural sources were no longer accepted as gospel truth.

The second change was in patterns of interaction. Jews sought recognition, acceptance, and friendship among non-Jews and referred to non-Jewish standards, manners and customs as a model for their own behavior. The fundamental identity of the Jews, rooted in Torah, culture, language and society was shattered.

As one went eastward, patches of humanism and secularism spread as well. The Enlightenment had its Jewish equivalent: the *Haskallah.* Borne by the *maskillim* — those who were "enlightened" — the new ways infiltrated the solid halachic way-of-life which Jews lived. Using classical Hebrew, the language of the Jewish elite, the *maskillim* developed a renewed though flowery Hebrew style. Their magazines and books brought the verities of the West into the hamlets, towns and cities of Eastern Europe.

A third reaction arose in time to offer an option between total assimilation (which meant the abandonment of Judaism) and walling Judaism into a closed rabbinic order. The third option sought ways in which Jews would remain Jewish and yet embrace ideas of freedom and

---

* The Count of Clermont-Tonnerre in the French National Assembly.

enlightenment. Within this new direction, a number of pathways opened.

REDEFINING RELIGIOUS IDENTITY IN THE WEST

One new form of Judaism, Reform, was fashioned by German Jews who were reeling in the face of new social possibilities and drunk with the taste of freedom and equality. The revolution that "Classic" Reform Judaism brought was its demotion of the Sabbath which, in some extreme instances, included exchanging the weekly day of rest, Saturday (Shabbat) for Sunday, the day of rest of the Gentile majority; abandonment of the Hebrew language as the tongue of prayer, and in general, formulation of a kind of Protestantized and "delandized" religion.* [Obviously, Classic Reform has been left far behind by today's Reform movement.]

Delandized Judaism is one in which the Holy Land, Eretz Israel, is a relic of the past, not a promise for the future. The early Reformers (Germans of the Mosaic persuasion) wanted to drop outlandish traditions and separatist "Oriental" behavior, as well as fidelity to the vision of a restored Land of Israel and the dream of the Return to Zion. These notions were deemed unacceptable to Christian gentlemen of reason, and therefore should be replaced by Western modes and mores. The reward was entree into the cultured salons of Berlin, as well as into the corridors of commerce and power.

In earlier days of the Emancipation, Jews had found it necessary to convert to be accepted fully into Christian society. The Mendelssohns, (descendants of Moshe Mendelssohn of Dessau, an Orthodox Jew and noted philosopher who was responsible for spreading the Enlightenment into myriads of Jewish homes) are a case in point, though, as their correspondence admits, "fully admitted" meant "not quite fully." Reform was a more dignified, less traitorous option: to remain Jewish and yet be German. Similar developments occurred in other Western European countries, and were carried by new migrants (especially those from Germany) to the New World.

Two other schools rose in Germany to face the promise and threat of the more open society. In reaction to Reform, but still in consonance

---

* I owe the word "delandized" to Professor Jacob Neusner.

with the social aspirations of the Jewish bourgeoisie, Rabbi Samson Raphael Hirsch (1808–1888) formulated a path which remained fully loyal ("Torah-true") to Halachah and tradition while admitting controlled change. Under the banner of *Torah im derech eretz,* that is, combining Torah (Halachah) with "worldly ways," Hirsch taught that the fully observant Jew might dress as the Germans did, engage in university and other secular studies, and use the German language for synagogue sermons. Hebrew however was the Holy Tongue and would remain the language of prayer and of the weekly reading of Bible and Prophets (Torah and Haftarah). This school, created in Frankfurt at mid-century, was called Neo-Orthodoxy.

Between the two — Reform and Neo-Orthodoxy — another approach was formulated, an attempt to wed strict Germanic scholarship, which had given Reform its theoretical basis, (the so called Science of Judaism, *Wissenschaft des Judentums*) with halachic observance. This approach was based on historic norms of religious practice. It was called the Historical School of Judaism and centered around the Jewish Theological Seminary of Breslau (then in Germany, and today's Wroclaw, Poland.)

These three movements shared a need to define Judaism as a religion, and Jewishness as belonging to a religious community based on common language and descent which resided in a majority Christian society that was inhospitable to Jews. They asserted their identity as a community of faith and religious practice.

None of the three movements drew the attention of the Gentiles to — indeed some actually tried to remove totally — the concept of the Jews as a separate people or nation. Their identity was essentially defined in religious terms. The message to their neighbors was, "We are German (or French) just as you are; it is only that we worship the One God in different ways." At best, they related a sense of peoplehood and the restoration of Zion to a time long past or to a vague and far-off future, a Messianic time when Israel would rejoin the family of nations. Classic Reform, unlike its modern and revised descendant, dropped the concept of the return to Zion altogether. This attitude, in varying degrees, colored the perceptions of the two other schools, even those which held that the Messianic era, or the Messiah, should indeed be prayed for daily, though "the latter days" are far off in a mystic time-to-come. The latter days are thus postponed indefinitely.

JEWISH IDENTITY IN EASTERN EUROPE

Westernized Jewry might have sought acculturation, if not actual assimilation, but Eastern Jewry was a very different community. Jews in the eastern reaches of the Austro-Hungarian Empire, in Czarist lands and in Poland and Rumania lived for the most part in multi-ethnic and multi-lingual societies. Religion and nationality were often, perhaps usually, one and the same.

There are some tragically fascinating examples. The Ukrainian-speaking people are called "Ukrainian" when they are Russian Orthodox, but Ruthenian if they practice the Catholic Eastern Rite. The Serbs and the Croats speak Serbo-Croatian, but the Serbs are Russian Orthodox and use the Cyrillic or Russian alphabet. The Croats are Catholic and write in Latin characters.

The Jews were Yiddish-speaking, Hebrew-praying and part of the Jewish people. The dream of freedom and equality, where it took hold, took on an immediate Messianic but anti-religious cast. The Messiah could come tomorrow if. . . if we were social revolutionaries. . . if we were socialists, communists. . . if we were Zionists. . . .

Most solutions sought by the Jews were based on their national identity, and attempted to marry their particular ideology to Jewish peoplehood. The major exceptions were the early Social Revolutionaries and subsequently the Communists who foresaw that "after the Revolution" there would be a new dawn of freedom and the rise of a social order in which national distinctions would fall away. But even among the Communists, there were a handful who maintained their Jewish identity and language, some of whom paid for this with their lives.

The bulk of Eastern European Jewry was clearly Jewish in its nationality; this was true for Russia and Poland, Latvia, Lithuania and Estonia, Romania, Bulgaria, Serbia and Austro-Hungary. These pre-World War I terms are used because that is when most of the Jewish communities of the New World were formed and the foundation laid for the Yishuv — the Jews of Palestine who were to build the ideological and material base for the State of Israel. Thus, broadly speaking, there was a dividing line between East and West in Jewish Europe. In the East, Jewish identity was defined as a nationality; Jews were a nation.

RELIGION IN THE WEST — NATIONALITY IN THE EAST

In brief, and as a generalization, the Western Jewish communities redefined their Jewishness as a religious identity. This permitted them to continue to associate as Jews within the framework of a liberal state. Jews in the East saw themselves as a national group within multi-cultural and multi-national empires.

In this sense, Israel is heir to Eastern European Jewry; America is the successor to Western Europe. The difference is not to be minimized. The dialogue between Israel and the Diaspora is confused by this basic difference. Israelis see themselves as part of a Jewish nation.

Zionism arose as a national response in the East, by those Jews who naturally saw themselves as part of a nation-people (the terms are interchangeable in the East.) But for Western Jews, Zionism was not simply a return to a national Jewish identity. It was a turning away from Western society's inability to make good the promise of emancipation and full equality, never fully realized and culminating in the Holocaust. It was anti-Semitism that turned the Westernized early Zionists, Hess, Pinsker and Herzl toward the nationalist solution.*

And here is a paradox of history: American Jewry and for that matter most Western Jewish communities are descendants of Jews who hail from Eastern Europe. In Latin and North America we must add to those of Eastern European origin, Jews who came from the Middle East. Both categories (Eastern European and Middle East) defined their identity in their countries of origin as national. Not so in their new home countries.

In the U.S., the loss of this sense of *national* identity was a question of time. In the early part of the century, Justice Louis B. Brandeis could still use the term "nationality" to describe American Jews. But more and more, national identity had to be dressed in religious forms. Thus,

---

* Moses Hess was born in 1812 in Germany, and wrote a pre-Herzlian book, *Rome and Jerusalem*, published in 1862; (d. 1875). Leo Pinsker, a Russian physician (1821–1891) wrote *Auto-Emancipation* in 1882, which also anticipated Herzl's *Judenstaat* (1891).

"peoplehood, coreligionists, ethnic community," replaced "nationality, national identity."

Nationality in Israel blends the ideology of the Eastern European founders with the new identity of the country, as Sephardi Jews similarly saw themselves as part of a nation-people. Add to these the *sabras* (the native-born) of all origins, who are brought up in a natural environment of national identity, and an inevitable cleavage in self-identity between Israeli and Diaspora Jew becomes apparent.

A further paradox. The non-Orthodox Jews of the West clung to a religious identity, among other reasons, to make themselves acceptable to their hosts. In Israel, an opposite dynamic: heirs to a vehement anti-Orthodoxy have created a stronghold of Orthodoxy.

THE SECULARISM OF THE FOUNDING FATHERS OF ISRAEL

Why were Israel's founding fathers so anti-Orthodox? Some the reasons follow:

the anti-clericalism of the Enlightenment versus the obscurantism of the rabbis;

the political activism of radicals against the passivism of the believer;

the restless search for science, knowledge, and "progress" that characterized the 19th century crashing against the rock-like defensiveness of a threatened Orthodoxy which adopted the rule that "innovation is prohibited by the Torah";*

Zionist fervor and belief in the need for Jews to take their fate into their own hands confronting the doctrine that not Man but Divine intervention will bring the Messiah and the restoration of Zion;

and, socialist atheism — note Marx's statement that "religion is the opiate of the people" — versus belief in God, the revealed Torah and Oral Law.

---

* The Hatam Sofer (1762–1839), the leading Ashkenazi arbiter of Halachah so ruled and his followers created walls buttressed from generation to generation.

But the stream of modern, socialist immigrants from Eastern Europe who could follow in the ideological steps of the founders was choked off by the British in the 1930s. In the 1940s, it was closed off — sealed and entombed in the graveyards of the Holocaust. The Ashkenazi ultra-Orthodox remnant closed ranks, built schools, and a remarkable self-contained social service network. It successfully recruited some of the Sephardi Orthodox. It created an enviable access to the financial resources of its overseas members who had achieved considerable success in business. The ultra-Orthodox birthrate — birth control is generally frowned upon — is easily triple that of the non-Orthodox, and thus the community increased rapidly, geometrically. Thus the ultra-Orthodox minority, for all its cleavages, built well and used Israel's chaotic political system to the best advantage, both in terms of state budgets and political power.

The paradox has dialectic symmetry; a classic and tragic joke that history plays on ideology. Nationalist Israel is hostage to Orthodoxy. America, the pluralistic nation which separates religion from state, views its Jews, and they view themselves, in religious terms.

POTENTIAL CHANGES IN THE WEST

Demographically, the United States contains within it its own Third World: a rising tide of dispossessed blacks, Hispanics fleeing Mexico's poverty, Central American and Caribbean upheavals and tragedies, Latin America's uncertainties. How will this affect the United States, educationally, politically, economically? Will the Oriental new Americans displace the Jews as the brain elite? Will the no-longer-marginal American Jew fade into the tangle of "white majority" Americans? Will Third World and Black Islamic anti-Semitism permit this, prevent it, or encourage it? Will the United States under social and economic tensions become so right-wing that Jews will feel uncomfortable living there? Will a Jesse Jackson or Buchanan ever come to power? Can real anti-Semitism become a power in future left- or right-wing government? Will Jews be displaced from their favored position in American life? Will an American government ever strike an anti-Israeli role which would force American Jews to rethink their status? Will Japan and the Pacific rim displace American superiority and if so, how will

American Jews feel about living in a second-class country? If Europe ever succeeds in uniting — what will that mean for the United States?

How will these possible developments influence Jews in other countries? Today, there is an Americanization of Jewish life in the non-U.S. Diaspora. Will that be the role model? Or will Europe in turmoil and the rise within it of the anti-Semitic right-wing require a different reaction?

And finally, how many Jews outside of Israel will, a generation from now, be sufficiently identified with, rooted in, and committed to their Jewishness? How at home will they be with a new kind of Israeli Jewishness, rooted in a perception of belonging to a nation and land, speaking differently from them, experiencing differently: not simply Jews but Israeli Jews?

CHAPTER FIFTEEN

A DAILY PLEBISCITE: AN ACT OF WILL

Of making many books there is no end, and much study is a weariness of the flesh.   — *Ecclesiastes* 11: 12

Etre une nation, c'est un plébiscite de tous les jours.
— Ernest Renan

In the past to stop being a Jew usually required doing something: conversion to another religion, abjuration, baptism. Today, especially in America and in the Americanizing West, to remain Jewish requires doing something. One can blend into the foliage of undistinguishable existence by doing nothing, just by being part of the mass culture and civil religion. To be a Jew consumes energy: it may require thought, a different lifestyle, different interests, or food habits. It may force one to spend money for membership in an organization or congregation, or to compel children to attend lessons they may not want. It may require forgoing leisure time to "be active" in communal life.

What keeps people Jewish, then? Ultimately an act of will. It is true that those who carry heavier baggage may find it harder to discard. People in the Satmar hasidic enclave in Williamsburg, or active academics around the yeshivot and seminaries, or children of leading Jewish figures in their communities are imbued with a lifestyle they may want to continue. Or, simply, their name makes assimilation harder, and so they just go on being — nominally, in both senses — Jews. And yet they may not. The less committed the immediate environment or subculture in which they live, the more chance of ceasing to be an identified Jew. Ultimately to be a Jew in the Diaspora is to want to be a Jew.

Ernest Renan, the French philosopher and philologist said over a hundred years ago, "To be a people is a daily plebiscite." Some come with a predisposition to say yes in the plebiscite. One can vote oneself "in" or simply drop out.

168

There are still highly committed Jews to be found in synagogues and temples: Reconstructionist, Reform, Conservative, Orthodox and ultra-Orthodox, as well as in *havurot* — informal prayer and study groups — of varying shades. They are found in secularist and leftist Jewish groupings. They may be active in fundraising, for local and Israeli institutions. The active leaders in these causes often form an interlocking directorate, in which "active" in one means active in many. They frequently live in a Jewish American sub-culture which to some extent provides a civil religion and an existential reality different from the mass culture, and from undefined "Americanism." These are the Jews who "carry" the sense of a united Jewish peoplehood, who live out their act of will, and vote in the daily plebiscite of identity. This vote is a statement, tacit or voiced, of their sense of unity of destiny. They cannot separate themselves from the body of the Jewish people, mystical though this may sound.

But do even they share a universe of discourse with their fellow-Jews in Israel? Do non-Orthodox Jews share a common universe of discourse with ultra-Orthodox? If peoplehood involves an act of identification, a shared culture and a sense of common destiny, how far do these go in the face of lack of a common language, and of vast differences in cultural milieu, civil religion and existential reality?

What of Israel? What act of will, if any, is required to be a Jew? "We have to educate ourselves that a People is not a religious sect, it is not an ideological movement that is supposed to march in step. . ."* This statement, by Professor Avi Ravitzky of the Hebrew University should be read in conjunction with what Sir Isaiah Berlin said in an interview published in *The Jerusalem Report.***

> Normalization — that is the proper purpose of the Zionist movement. I'm not particularly interested when people say, "The Jews are a wonderful nation. They should be a source of

---

* From Conversation with Avi Ravitzky in "Jew and Jew" in *Scopus*, Magazine of the Hebrew University of Jerusalem , Volume 38, Summer 1988, p. 37.
** *The Jerusalem Report*, "Limited Premier Edition," October 1990, "Reflections of a Zionist Don," an interview by Rochelle Furstenberg, pp. 50-51. Emphasis added.

light unto the nations. . . ." I'm perfectly content if they're a nation like other nations not particularly distinguished. I sincerely hope they're marvelous. But even if they're not. . . . *[Israel is] Jewish if it contains Jews, their habits, their values, their goals, their relationship to each other.*

Jews who have a sense of *national identity*, and a feeling of being a minority — an *exiled* minority — require a state:

> "National" means that people are conscious of belonging to a nation. . . . [Late eighteenth-century philosopher J.G. von Herder]. . . spelled it out. "People need to drink. They need to eat. They need shelter, they need security, liberty, justice, *and they need to belong.*" If you take this away they are in exile. *And exile is a wound.* . . .
>
> Of course, without persecution there would have been no Zionism at all. But that wasn't what impinged on me particularly. *I always felt I was a Russian Jew,* not a Russian, not from Riga, *but a Russian Jew.*

Sir Isaiah's statement shows clearly the national sense of belonging which is a basic attribute of Eastern European Jews. Beyond this, he uses the word *nation,* **not** *people,* to describe the Jews. In this sense, the Israeli Jewish population is that part of the people which is forming a nation. There is no question about their Jewishness. You can argue that this is a bare minimum, that people are not aware of their Jewishness, or do not live up to an ideological standard, or a religious code.

Whatever one's views, the realities of life makes all in Israel Jews. Even the Arab citizens of Israel have a bit of a "Jewish" lifestyle: the basic calendar and rhythm of life, just as American Jews on the whole live by an internal clock and calendar which is not Jewish. Furthermore, all residents of Israel share a unity of destiny which expresses itself in strange, sometimes bizarre terms. During the Gulf War, just as Scud missiles did not differentiate between Jew and Arab, so certainly did they not distinguish between Jew and Jew. All sat in sealed rooms.

Ultra-Orthodox Jews in Israel willy-nilly share that sense of destiny: they either accept it, rebel against it, or try to ignore it. But they cannot — in the ultimate sense or in the practical — live without an awareness of this. From those who hate the State and work against it in public ways, to those who coexist within the framework, the State of Israel determines one of their key frames of reference, in Renan's words, that of *tous les jours*, of the mundane and day-to-day. Ultimately, *ultimately*, if Jewish blood is shed, they cannot simply ignore it.

This daily contact with the State and society is enhanced in times of danger. During the Gulf War, in a tongue-in-cheek, yet somehow awed report in Israel's most widely read daily newspaper, there is a description of a Cabalistic rite enacted to "strengthen our people."* Ten *tzadikim* — righteous men — conducted an occult ceremony, black candles, prayer-shawls, ancient bans and curses. In a cave near the birthplace of the prophet Samuel, as a haredi response to Saddam's war, the ten righteous men launched a curse to destroy Saddam. They were instigated by one of the leaders of a part of the anti-Zionist, anti-Israel Netorei Karta.

What was this? Was it an attack using weapons they possessed to save only haredim from Scud attacks? Was it not really a prayer-launch to save Jews of all kinds, that is, Israel the people? Was it even an act of spiritual war to save Israel the State? Whatever the intention, at that moment certainly there was unity of destiny tying together Netorei Karta and the rest of Israel, though the rest of Israel — the majority — preferred to rely on other types of launches.

And even the journalist, trying to distance himself from the act, could not but express his sense of history and unity of destiny in his final sentences. "And all this took place in Jerusalem, 2577 years after the destruction of the First Temple, 2553 years after the death of Nebuchanezzar, the Evil Man of Iraq. And CNN called to hear how it went."

Jews in the Diaspora who share this sense of unity of destiny are part of the Jewish people, an adjunct to the nation of Israel. But for most, that unity of destiny is shared at times of peaks of ecstasy or of fear. The day-to-day, the mundane, is on another plane: a civil religion and an existential reality so far removed as to present an historic divide, a watershed. Once this is recognized, it is certainly not final. To change it pits the individual and collective will against the force of historic development.

---

* *Shiv'ah Yamim* [Seven Days], the week-end magazine of *Yediot Aharonot*, Tel Aviv, February 8, 1991, p. 24.

REBUILDING UNITY

> ... but the triple cord is not easily broken.
> — *Ecclesiastes* 4:12

Many ingrained myths and conventional truths have been reexamined in this book, in an effort to expose the danger that the Jews are becoming three peoples. Disagreement will come from many involved and committed Jews, Israelis, Diasporites and ultra-Orthodox. It challenges basic assumptions, "self-evident truths:" of course, it will be argued, of course the Jews are one people. Jews are Jews.

Certainly the non-Jew with no axe to grind, and most certainly the anti-Semite will usually lump all Jews together. There is a Hebrew saying that all the Greek race have the same face.* It could well be applied by an outsider looking in on the Jews. "Whatever differences you Jews claim to have among yourselves, you're all different from us, you're simply Jews."

The thesis of this book runs counter to these self-evident truths and conventional slogans. Entire establishments numbering thousands of lay leaders and professionals — fund-raising movements, Zionist organizations, political pressure committees, religious and philanthropic groups — all base themselves on the slogan, and in most cases on the belief that We are One. However, to serve as a chart for the future, ideology must be based on the correct topography of the present.

Slogans which have become conventional truths are therefore enemy number one of ideology. What may have been true at one time, or at one place becomes a total world-view, which does not change when time and place change, as they inexorably must. Political Zionism began with an accurate assessment of the situation of the Jews of Eastern and Central Europe. The reading was based on the realities of the late 19th century.

A new reading of reality is needed: "We are One" — possibly. We are in danger of — probably in the process of — becoming three. Other-

---

* *Lechol ha-yevanim, otam ha-panim,* cf. "All Orientals look alike".

wise we live the conventional truth, which is often the conventional lie. The outstanding intellectual of the early Zionist movement was Dr. Max Nordau, a writer and thinker much more famous in his time than Herzl. One of Nordau's books was called *The Conventional Lies of Our Civilization.**

If the establishments recognize the need to examine conventional lies, and if individual Jews realize this, to some extent the process of drift and schism may be halted — all other things being equal. What do we mean, "all other things being equal?" In the previous chapter, we raised a number of hypothetical, and perhaps not-so-hypothetical questions about the future. If some or many of these occur, present reality changes; "all other things" will no longer be equal. The unknown future will reveal itself and may, or more precisely must change our premises. Until then, we must act if want the Jewish people to continue its peoplehood in some semblance of unity.

For Jews to maintain their unity, a network of velvet chains and silken cords must bind them. The Thirteen Colonies were well on their road to independence from Britain when "social communication (that is trade, travel, correspondence and the like)" were greater among themselves than between them and the mother country. No realist can expect American or Diaspora Jews to make themselves independent of their home countries, nor do they wish to do so. We can only tie them to us and us to them through interlocking our lives, families, friendships, languages, universe of discourse, studies, travel, commerce and investments.

LEARNING AND A UNIVERSE OF DISCOURSE

Specific things. Real things. Not just conferences, and declarations and pomp and ceremony. Recognizing that we have no longer a common (religious) universe of discourse, we must make learning a major

---

* Nordau (1849–1923) was a fascinating and brilliant man for all seasons. Born in Pest, Hungary, he became a medical doctor, but gained fame and notoriety as a philosopher and writer. He was Herzl's Vice-President of the World Zionist Organization, and is considered its co-founder. His analyses of world trends and thought led him to predict at the Zionist Congress of 1911 the danger of extinction for six million Jews. *Conventional Lies. . .* was first published in Leipzig 1883, translated, Chicago, 1884.

Jewish aim. We must reward Jewish literacy with prestige and roles of leadership. Jewish illiteracy is not just a Diaspora attribute. The Israeli press reports that "Jewish studies programs in the nation's secular schools. . . were totally inadequate." * The failure of Israel's secular school system in this area is disappointing. Nonetheless, for all the "inadequacy" of Jewish studies, more Jews live and breathe Jewish knowledge in Israel than outside of it. If the Diaspora non-Orthodox, and the world-wide Orthodox and ultra-Orthodox are to recreate a key element of universal Jewish dialogue, it requires the less knowledgeable to work at learning the basics of Jewish history and the texts of its literary, especially Biblical-Talmudical, or, if you insist, "religious" heritage. As Ben Gurion said, "Not books *about* the Bible! *The Bible!*"

Israel, since it is a state, can do much more about this than voluntary communities. Ultimately, the government and the Knesset can enforce this, provided public opinion is not too hostile. Some "State" (non-Orthodox) schools are conducting special programs to strengthen Jewish content. A promising sign both of openness on the Orthodox side and the desire of parents for more content is the establishment of a number of schools in Jerusalem which do not examine the practices of their pupils' parents; that is, non-Orthodox parents are welcome to have their children study in them. There are a number of Conservative (*Mesorati–*Traditional) schools throughout the country, and the Reform have opened a school in Jerusalem as well.

Most important, Diaspora Jews who wish to enter into the soul of Judaism and Jewishness must know Hebrew. Those who seek to carry the beauty of the Jewish past into the future and at the same time to maintain close ties to Israel cannot do so without the language. The case has been stated powerfully by Nessa Rapoport, a young writer who lives in New York.**

> . . . to think about the learning and teaching of Hebrew in this
> country [the United States] is to confront some of Judaism's

---

* The Jerusalem Post, "Secular schools flunk Jewish studies," March 12, 1991, p. 2.
** Excerpts from "In Living Hebrew" by Nessa Rapoport, *Hadassah* Magazine, New York, October, 1990, Volume 72, Number 2, p. 30.

most critical questions: What has united us as a people? Do we need a universal Jewish language? Is it possible to be a serious Jew without knowing Hebrew — a people of the book only in translation? Can an elite minority — the relatively few Hebrew readers and speakers here — transmit culture? And can culture save us?

As with all important issues, the political is also personal. Why was I already obsessed by the question of which Jewish day school would best teach my not-yet-two-year-old son the Hebrew skills and facility that my own day school, for all its faults, had bequeathed to me? Why did I care about Hebrew first, before any other element in his Jewish education? . . .

What has Hebrew given me? Everything from the ephemeral to the sublime. It enabled me to play the lead in a Hebrew production of Heidi at camp, for example: No small matter when you're 11. It allowed me to step off a plane in 1971 and feel as at home in Jerusalem that first time as if I'd always lived there. No small matter even now. At my most mystical I confess to seeing a word of Hebrew as a drop of blood: Within the microcosm, one can decode the structure of life itself and the crucial information about the organism. When an Israeli soccer game ends in a tie, the referee declares teiku — the Talmudic acronym for *Tishbi yetaretz kushiyot u-ve'ayot* (Elijah will resolve difficulties and problems), which is how the rabbis concluded an argument in which neither side was victorious. . .

Coming away from a vision of mobilizing American Jews to value and cultivate the Hebrew language, I can say this: If you want to taste the real thing, Hebrew is it. No Jew who has read the Torah in Hebrew will call it the Old Testament again.

If you want to fall in love with where you come from, Hebrew is it. This is the language your ancestors dreamed in and died for.

If you want your children to feel passionately about being Jews, give them the key. If they don't learn to use it when they're young, not only won't they know Hebrew but they'll be translating Jewish values, too, and diluting them in the process. For a language and its values are not separable. A *brit* is more than a covenant; *tzedakah* is more than charity; a *brakha* is more than a blessing. . .

Hebrew in the Diaspora remains in exile, remains the possession of that "elite minority" — often an elite only in the eyes of themselves and other, especially Israeli, Hebrew-speakers.

Is the plea for Hebrew just another pious wish, a bow to the required conventions of those who write about Jewish continuity? It dare not be. *The Hebrew language and familiarity with Jewish tradition and its books are the sine qua non,* without which all is a mockery, a pale image in a fading mirror. If being Jewish is an act of will, a conscious choice, it cannot be so smothered in sugar as to become a placebo. Learning is the base of Jewishness.

EXILE AND HOME*: GALUT AND BAYIT

Sir Isaiah Berlin said that if you take away from people their sense of *belonging,* they are in exile. The opposite of Exile (Galut), in Hebrew thought, is Redemption (Geulah). But it seems that today's generation in the West has abandoned the search for Redemption. If Jews do not know they are in exile, why should they search?

On a practical level, "exile" means not being at home, not living in your own homeland. "Home" (*Bayit*) is the opposite of exile. To try to tell American or most Diaspora Jews that they are in exile is rampant nonsense. Their existential reality tells them differently. But for many such Jews, living in Israel, vicariously or temporarily, may be a living dynamic demonstration of "Home:" a transition from being a member of a "religious" group and a minority to living as part of a national majority in a totality of Jewishness.

Young and old may find a sympathetic cord vibrate within themselves when in Israel. The visit may arouse the sense of being at home, of being a *Ba'al ha-bayit,* in simple language, a householder, and more precisely "Master of the House."

---

* We are indebted to Professor Avi Ravitzky of the Hebrew University for refining for us in a number of lectures the concept of "Home" as an alternative to exile, and a modern replacement for the word "Redemption."

(The greatest enemy of this, a knowledgeable Israeli observer of Israel-Diaspora relations points out paradoxically, is "the mission to Israel." He explicitly referred to "mega-missions," in which hundreds of people come to Israel for a few days in the framework of fundraising organizations, in order to whip up their enthusiasm and open their checkbooks. These missions usually play up emotional highlights of the moment: immigrants arriving, military bases, whatever is "hot" at the time. They leave little or no time for meeting Israelis, of talking with peers, of sensing "home." They are "quick-fix" trips, what he called an "instant show." Israel is a fundraising tool, rather than an end in itself. Though valuable perhaps as openers, these missions are often the only — and skewed — sighting of Israel for many.)

Obviously, a Diaspora Jewish family which lived in Israel for a few months, as part of the people, would initially experience a sense of strangeness. But eventually, as happened with many such families, the sense of being at home would prevail. Just as obviously, to hope that most Diaspora families would do this is a pious wish, totally incapable of being realized. Some have done it, some undoubtedly will, but most, the overwhelming most, will not! But young people could.

We must change the priorities in "other" Jewish people, the Diaspora Jews. Figures presented to the Jewish Agency in the second half of the 1980s showed that only 45,000 young Jews a year from all over the world come to Israel on a tour or visit or study program. The statistics of Jews from the United States who have visited Israel are supposedly less than 20%. In spite of the tradition of pilgrimage, the ease and relative cheapness of travel, the exhortations of rabbis and efforts of pro-Israeli organizations, the figures are extremely low. Diaspora Jew simply do not understand the importance Israelis attach to this.

An example. There have been two periods of deep existential Israeli Jewish loneliness in the last few decades — the waiting period before the Six-Day War of 1967, and the Iraqi Scud attacks. During the Scud War, Diaspora Jews in their masses stayed away from Israel. Unity of destiny? A Canadian student at the Hebrew University, Jonathan Shiff, had this to say about Diaspora Jews during the Scud period.

Nothing deepened my understanding of the people more than
the Gulf War. . . . I now feel — rather than know — how and

why Israelis see Diaspora Jews and the relationship between the two communities.

As we lined up for gas masks and tried them on, students here for the year and other tourists began to leave. When the deadline approached, I experienced, for the first time, something that Diaspora Jews never feel: the atmosphere of war. Friends of mine — especially pilots — disappeared into reserve duty, and others were on standby. None of us could concentrate on school, and everything seemed to be suspended in mid-air.

And all the while, the airport was filled with foreigners streaming out. With one or two exceptions, the "solidarity missions" escaped before the war started, and the streets of Jerusalem felt empty. Even the leaders of the Jewish Agency refused to come to Israel for a meeting, a symbolic act which, for me, spoke louder than all the cheques and plaques and declarations in the world.

Thus, I purposely used the word "foreigners." I, who hold only a Canadian passport, felt estranged from Diaspora Jews. Maybe they are my cousins, they are certainly not my brothers and sisters. When I sit in my sealed room at 3 a.m. with my gas mask on, hearing the sirens wail and listening to the radio, I have more in common with the Kurdish woman in South Tel Aviv than I do with the friends I grew up with.

In a sense, you could put it this way: North American Jews and I share a past, and we probably have more to talk about together than I do with many people here. But Israelis and I share a present and a future. We are building that future together, weighing options, making decisions, burying our dead and celebrating our joys. This is sharpened when we are at war, precisely because other Jews are not at war.

Those same Jewish leaders will return after the war to present us with checks and suggest how to run our country. I respect their right to express themselves, and don't doubt their sincerity. But like other Israelis, I will probably just shake my head and not take them seriously at all.

A well-planned and well-financed effort to get thousands upon thousands of young single Jews, students at universities and colleges, and thousands of young married couples to spend time in Israel could make the difference. Finally, only recently, the organized American community and a major Jewish foundation have begun to organize youth tours on a broader basis.

Similarly, Jewish people in their middle years should be encouraged to spend a "sabbatical" in Israel. The word sabbatical is bound in quotation marks because the intention is not just teachers who are entitled to such study periods. It should be extended to all professionals in Jewish organizations, and at the expense of their employers. Jewish leaders or would-be activists should also have sabbaticals in Israel, whether self-financed or subsidized by a fund for that purpose.

BRIDGES OVER THE OCEAN

One potential but sturdy bridge between the Diaspora and Israel is a narrow one indeed: the bridge of people, the *olim* or emigrants who leave the West to make their homes in Israel. Obviously, the most visible reservoir of potential olim from the West are people who choose to live in Israel for "positive" reasons, that is, to strengthen their Jewish identity, to erase the hyphen from that identity, to live among a Jewish majority in whatever religious or ideological ambience they may choose. This would apply to both the Orthodox and those who come out of an ideological commitment of another sort, mainly members of Zionist youth movements which indoctrinate toward aliyah.

The two groups either seek religious identity, or national identity, while some combine the two. On occasion, neither ideology is the moving factor, but just the desire to "feel at home" or to "be Jewish."

Retirees may find Israel a temporary haven or a place of solace for their twilight years. What a cord pulling families to Israel this would be — children and grandchildren coming to spend time with their elders?

There are two underlying principles. The first, discussed above, is to live the sense of Home, to revive it, so that perhaps the sense of Exile will appear, *de facto*, as a lesson of life. The other is to create human links which are deep and real. For that reason, *aliyah*, settling in Israel is a true and real nexus. The families of the immigrants, their friends, their schoolmates and neighbors can identify Israel with a person, with an individual whose fate and life are important to them, or have been important to them.

Personal ties with Israel on all levels are vital if we are to retie the thrice-knotted cord. The sociologist we mentioned in connection with the Thirteen Colonies has shown this clearly. Ben Gurion understood it well.* In addition to studying, visiting or living temporarily in Israel, there are newer routes which the official organizations have not fully explored.

A HOME IN ISRAEL

Israel as Home, as opposed to Exile, can best be realized by Jews buying a home in Israel. But a home here is more than a symbol. It is a statement, and on a practical level a tangible attraction to be used, to be lived in. This need not be the preferred route of the rich only. People of lesser means could share in buying apartment after apartment, by pooling their funds: a more practical and efficient exercise in Zionism than speech-making and deciding on the future of the territories they will not inhabit anyway. A home-in-Israel club in a synagogue or neighborhood would be another vital link, among the participants themselves and between them and Israel.

This could also be a step to what might be called "partial aliyah." Most active businessmen and corporate officials cannot easily give up their professions and occupations in middle-age. Yet, given today's instantaneous communications: modem-linked computers, faxes, telephones, satellite hookups and the like, some might just as well spend a certain number of months in Israel with no damage to their careers. The gains for the individual, the family, and the nexus are clear.

And finally, trade and investments. The old saw is outdated, the one which, at the time rather accurately said, "You know how to make a small fortune in Israel? Bring a large one!" Israel has many successful businessmen, and a number of overseas investors have done well here. In this non-ideological age, trade and investment may count for more than preaching and theory. True, some investors or trading partners may become disaffected or disenchanted, but in the main even they developed deep personal ties. Frequent trips here may lead to partial

---

* See *BEN GURION, State-Builder*, cited, pp. 242 ff.

aliyah or owning a home here, and thus shift the center of gravity for the investor's family. This could lead to some knowledge of Hebrew and greater understanding of and identification with the people of Israel. And the bonus might even be to succeed in making money!

Again, this need not be only the purview of the rich. Middle income groups can for example set up investment clubs for people without much capital, in community centers and synagogues. Merchants could pool to import Israeli goods and build a network of personal contacts with Israel at the same time. These would be practical actions in a language which today's pragmatists understand. It must be a grass roots effort. Unfortunately, "official" Diaspora-Israel relations are in the hands of politicians in Israel, and of Diaspora leaders most of whom have other, often important, agendas. A true ideological discussion and clarification is impossible as long as Diaspora leadership remains "unideological" and Israeli leadership pursues its own agendas. The major interest of Israel's establishment is to benefit from the political support of Diaspora Jewry.

One important area neglected by both sets of power brokers is the synagogue and the spiritual connection. Jews cannot be Jews without either being religious or knowing enough to rebel against religion. The first Rabbi Kook is reported to have said, "It is not heretics (*apikorsim*) I fear, it is ignoramuses (*am ha-aratzim*) I fear."* Though the synagogue has not had great success in transmitting faith, tradition, or knowledge, it is at least dedicated to them, and thus possesses kernels of hope. The intensive use of a synagogue for Hebrew classes, study groups, *as well as "Buy-your-Home-in-Israel" clubs as well as "Invest-in-Israel" clubs can give the synagogue or temple a new dynamism, and give Israel a base for its relations with the Diaspora outside of the politicized or fund-raising agendas of federations and pressure groups.*

Will this stem the tide? Probably not. The close ones will grow closer and the distant, with exceptions which often colorfully prove the

---

* The Hebrew *Apikores* (pl. *apikorsim*), is a Hebraized form of the name Epicurus, the Greek philosopher, from which English borrowed the adjective "Epicurean." Yosef Zuriel, journalist and writer reminded me of the phrase. The Hebrew verb for "I fear" is reflexive: I fear, and also, as it were, fear for myself. It is a strong expression, and shows that Hebrew must be known to begin to grasp the full force of what is being said.

rule, will grow more distant. The bulk of the identified may very well sink into the comfort of day-to-day life. Not assimilation, but "death by a kiss," just doing nothing. . . .

What then will happen? Will we continue the present trend of division, distance and separation? Is it inevitable that we become three different peoples, recognizing a vague association, drifting apart, and eventually part of us disappearing, or at most nodding vaguely at each other as we walk down the road of the future?

This book was written to warn of that danger. Recognizing it, Jews will have to make their choices: Israelis to see Jewish destiny as affecting not only residents of the State, but all Jews. To negate the Galut, yes, but not to negate the *golim*, those who live in that Diaspora-Exile.*

And what of the nexus between ultra-Orthodox, Orthodox and non-Orthodox or secular? Can these universes of discourse be repaired or restored?

In the short run, there is only one way to avoid widening the breach. First, all must recognize that the danger-point has been reached. That recognition should force all three major religious trends to back off: to declare, in the name of Jewish peoplehood and unity, a cease-fire, a moratorium on civil war. Though each group claims a monopoly on truth, whether that truth is Halachah or, if each pursues its present course, we are on the brink of — or perhaps have already passed the point of mutual *de facto* excommunication.

Ultra-Orthodoxy must be convinced that in preserving itself by increasing material and politic short-term benefits, it will create a wall not to protect itself, but to cut itself off from Knesset Yisrael, the totality of the Jewish people. Liberal Judaism and secular Jews must be convinced that in answering concerns of the present, they may be helping erect greater and higher barriers to a unified Jewish people in the future. It may be very much "liberal" and very little "Jewish."

Among the ultra-Orthodox and Orthodox groups, as certainly within the liberal and secular elements, there are many Jews who believe we must live side-by-side with our Arab neighbors in peace and harmony. Are these same people so racist as not to wish to live in *de facto* har-

---

* "To negate the Exile, but not the exiled" is a phrase coined by Professor Eliezer Schweid.

mony and peace with their fellow-Jews? Those who are ready to negotiate with the PLO surely cannot refuse to seek unity with their Jewish brethren without preconditions: ultra- or Orthodox, Conservative, Reform or secular. And that may be the litmus test of the slogan of One Jewish People; the way to distinguish the political "religious leader" from the spiritual figures who will determine the continuity of one Jewish people into the future.

There may already be an irreparable breach over "Who is a Jew," over forms of marriage, intermarriage and patrilineal descent. Then the secularist Israelis may make common cause with the liberal Diaspora Jews, pushing the moderate Orthodox into the ultra-Orthodox camp. And even though the ultra-Orthodox in Israel, willy-nilly, share an apparent unity of destiny with other Israelis, their intransigent inability to compromise may make that breach an ugly war of attrition, or a chasm lined with total indifference. That would make two Jewish peoples an inevitable result.

But given the other breach in continuity and contact, between Israel and the Diaspora, the deep differences in the realities of day-to-day life and civil religion in a vacuum of common religious or linguistic ties, the third people may result. Only a great, an overwhelming individual and collective act of will can change this process.

A major psychological breakthrough will be needed, and massive self-restraint. The words "authentic" and "legitimate" will have to be used carefully. Israelis tell overseas Jews that only in Israel can they live authentically as Jews. Liberal Diaspora Jews judge ultra-Orthodoxy by its legitimacy in the liberal Western tradition. The ultra-Orthodox judge all others by the own legitimating value of Halachah and the inauthenticity of the lifestyle of the others. If all are equal, none is valid, that is true. But if we are to live as one in mutual respect and a desire to continue into the future, we need to find a kinder language with which to measure one another. When existence is at stake, moderation is an unwelcome guest. Without moderation, existence is threated with irreparable schism.

An act of self-control, and act of will may increase the saving remnant. . . . All else being equal.

When all is said and done, can any of these "remedies" cure the patient? Can seemingly immutable socio-historic forces be changed by an act of will? To me it seems certain that Jews who live in Israel will be Jewish and will hammer out, over the next generations, a new culture and a new society, possibly even a new vision for mankind. Those who join us — out of need , or better, out of desire — will ensure their future as Jews and that of their offspring.

Those who remain in the Diaspora face a constant struggle. Their success will generally be better ensured by structured religious patterns, deeper Jewish knowledge and close ties to Israel. They must choose between living in Israel and that struggle, recognizing the odds are against them.

Jewish tradition does not permit a liturgical reading to end on a note of chastisement or despair.* To close on a false note — upbeat, in today's usage — would however be blasphemy. Ultimately, it will depend on our faith in the life-drive of the Jewish people, and the guarantee of that will-to-life which Israel provides. Israel gives this will and faith expression, perspective, and — with all its back-sliding — hope.

A talented Israeli writer of startling creativity, David Grossman speaks of his view of Israel which can help make our destiny clearer.**

> One can live a responsible life in Iceland or Denmark, but it is easier there to avoid responsibility. Here you must cope every day with deep moral and practical questions, continually reformulate yourself, make personal choices that matter. I think that had I been born elsewhere I would have chosen to live in Israel. It offers such a personal challenge to a Jew. . . .
>
> I'm not one of those who say that if Arik Sharon becomes prime minister I will leave. No: it's my country exactly like Arik Sharon's country, and I will not leave the stage to others.
>
> I get offers all the time to spend a few years abroad. But I can't leave Israel, not even for a year. I don't want my children growing in an atmosphere other than Israel's. Not because of

---

* "All the prophets open with chastising and close with comforting. . . ." *Midrash Shoher Tov*, 4.

** In *The Jerusalem Report,* January 10, 1991, "The Possession of David Grossman" by Yossi Klein Halevi, p. 34.

provinciality; you can be provincial in Manhattan too. But I believe that taking part in this Israeli experiment is a privilege — yes, despite everything. I haven't lost the feeling that our being here is a miracle, that I write novels in a language that was practically dead a hundred years ago.

I am amazed by the vitality of the people here — despite our political paralysis. I don't find the same libido in other places. And that's what gives me hope. Once we are redeemed from this spell that we've put on ourselves, we can create a *Gan Eden*, a Garden of Eden. Alright [laughing], maybe that's too grandiose. A *Ganon Eden*, a little Garden of Eden.

A hundred years ago, visionaries understood that the lives of millions of Jews hung in the balance, that the life of an elemental unified Jewish people hung by a thread. Fifty years ago, after Hitler, one could easily have written *Finis* to the story of the Jews, just as one could have done in the year 70 of the Common Era when the Second Jewish Commonwealth was put to torch by the Romans.

· · ·

History is the joker in the sociologists' deck of cards. History is not immutable. It can be made — be changed — by individuals. If anything has proven that, the birth of Israel has proven it.

The dangers lie ahead.

So does the choice!

---

1. Karl Deutsch's theory was summarized by Professor Dankwart A. Rustow in *A World of Nations*, Washington, DC, the Brookings Institution, 1967. p. 61:

Nationality is not an inborn characteristic but the result of a process of social learning and habit forming. Such learning typically results from a marked increase of social communication (that is, of trade, travel, correspondence and the like), within a network linking a number of cities and each of these with its rural hinterland.

INDEX